Kidding around
IN
EAST SUSSEX

Len Markham

COUNTRYSIDE BOOKS
NEWBURY BERKSHIRE

◆ ◆

First published 2006
© Len Markham 2006

COUNTRYSIDE BOOKS
3 Catherine Road
Newbury, Berkshire

To view our complete range of books
please visit us at
www.countrysidebooks.co.uk

ISBN 1 85306 953 1
EAN 978185306 953 6

Designed by Peter Davies, Nautilus Design

Produced through MRM Associates Ltd., Reading
Typeset by Mac Style, Nafferton, E. Yorkshire
Printed by Borcombe Printers, Romsey

Contents

Kiddiwalks in East Sussex

◆◆◆◆◆◆◆◆◆◆◆◆◆◆◆◆◆◆◆◆◆◆◆◆◆◆◆◆◆◆◆◆◆◆◆◆◆

PUBLISHER'S NOTE

We hope that you obtain considerable enjoyment from this book; great care has been taken in its preparation. Although at the time of publication all routes followed public rights of way or permitted paths, diversion orders can be made and permissions withdrawn.

We cannot, of course, be held responsible for such diversion orders and any inaccuracies in the text which result from these or any other changes to the routes nor any damage which might result from walkers trespassing on private property. We are anxious though that all details covering the walks are kept up to date and would therefore welcome information from readers which would be relevant to future editions.

The simple sketch maps that accompany the walks in this book are based on notes made by the author whilst checking out the routes on the ground. However, for the benefit of a proper map, we do recommend that you purchase the relevant Ordnance Survey sheet covering your walk. The Ordnance Survey maps are widely available, especially through booksellers and local newsagents.

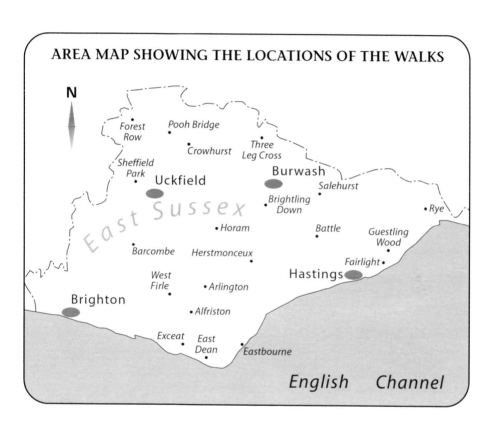

AREA MAP SHOWING THE LOCATIONS OF THE WALKS

N

Forest Row
Pooh Bridge
Crowhurst
Three Leg Cross
Sheffield Park
Uckfield
Burwash
Salehurst
East Sussex
Brightling Down
Rye
Horam
Battle
Guestling Wood
Barcombe
Herstmonceux
Fairlight
West Firle
Arlington
Hastings
Brighton
Alfriston
Exceat
East Dean
Eastbourne

English   Channel

Introduction

I was born to be a pedestrian. I was given a pair of leather bootees as a toddler and I've been a walker ever since. Walking was a necessity at first. Bus-fare money was reserved for half-yearly visits into town to get my hair cut, and besides, sixpence saved on such extravagances could buy you a bag of gobstoppers and several toffee bars that would keep you sucking for a week. I walked through the bombed out, back-to-back suburbs of a grim northern town at first but gradually, with the aid of a crumpled old map that had kept my fish and chips warm, I found a greener land, cool and beckoning. And that was it! I invested in a pair of boots and began to explore, eventually traversing thousands of miles of my native Yorkshire with my children by my side, recording my travels in a dozen or so walking books.

Since I came to live in Sussex, I've been spellbound at the gently rolling chalk Downs, the towering sea cliffs, the flint-built villages, the woodlands filled with flowers and the lush streamside meadows that inspired Rudyard Kipling to write this:

God gives all men all earth to love,
But since man's heart is small,
Ordains for each one spot shall prove
Beloved over all.
Each to his choice, and I rejoice
The lot has fallen to me
In a fair ground – in a fair ground –
Yea, Sussex by the sea!

Well, the glorious lot has fallen to me to write a book on exploring Kipling's beloved Sussex with children in mind and I do so with a leap and a bound.

In devising these routes, I'm obviously aware of the limitations of young legs so I've compromised … but only on the length of the routes and the nature of some of the climbs. My aim throughout has been to offer walks that provide all the excitement, stimulation, enjoyment, challenge and sense of achievement that walking books for adults provide.

Introduction

❖ ❖

The first fifteen of these tried and tested walks are less than three miles in length (although the routes from Firle and Three Leg Cross have a longer version if your party is feeling particularly energetic) and can be accomplished by the younger children – and their grandparents. Some of these walks are, where specified, suitable for toddlers and for buggies. The last five walks are a little more demanding. These, perhaps, may be reserved until the children have 'won their spurs'!

In these pages you'll find walks that take you into all sorts of delightful places, which it has been a joy to discover. Bluebell-filled woods, giddy clifftop heights, serene riverbanks, nature reserves ringing to the sound of rare birds, surf-lashed beaches and quiet villages – they're all here for every member of the family to enjoy.

Each walk in the book is presented in as user friendly a manner as possible. The routes, all circular, are briefly described and key information is given about locations, starting points, parking, mileages, time durations of walks and refreshment places. There is also a section headed 'Fun Things to See and Do' giving details of such attractions as zoos, museums and steam railways and opportunities for surfing, bike hire, river cruising, pooh-sticking and fishing. I've also appended background, walk-relevant notes to enhance the enjoyment of the routes.

The sketch maps that accompany each walk are meant as general guides but I do also recommend that parents invest in the quoted Ordnance Survey maps. These identify other fascinating features in the Sussex countryside and add to the enjoyment of the outing.

In these short pages I've really enjoyed getting to know a beautiful lady who, the experts would have us believe, has such a press of suitors that they clog every yard. But … do you know … in nearly one hundred miles … I hardly ever saw a soul. So then let us begin!

Len Markham

1

Eastbourne

Tiddly Om Pom Prom!

On the beach at Eastbourne

Glittering Eastbourne, the star of the sunshine coast, draws visitors by the thousand. They come to catch the rays and enjoy the simple pleasures of partaking in those good old British pastimes of loafing on the beach and ambling along the promenade to make room for the cream teas. Many of the visitors are in their twilight years but they still show an impressive turn of heel on a pancake flat walk with wonderful sea views and bracing airs. As a young person's introduction to the delights of walking, this amble on the so-called 'Pathway to Health' would be hard to beat and, on the outward stretch, it is suitable for pushchairs. Take grandpa's hand and off we go! The homeward path is on gravel but you have the option, during the holiday season, of returning along the outward route by Dotto Train.

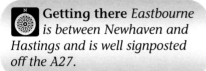 **Getting there** *Eastbourne is between Newhaven and Hastings and is well signposted off the A27.*

Length of walk $1^{1}/_{2}$ miles (returning by train) or 3 miles.
Time 1 or $2^{1}/_{2}$ hours.
Terrain Flat and level all the way there, with one short ascent to a flat and level gravelled return path.
Start/Parking Start at Eastbourne Pier (GR 618988). There are numerous free on-street parking places (some time restricted) in the town and several pay and display zones. Toilet facilities are available at Holywell.
Map OS Explorer 123 Eastbourne and Beachy Head.
Refreshments The Holywell Café at the halfway point offers lunches and snacks. Telephone: 01323 601598.

The Walk

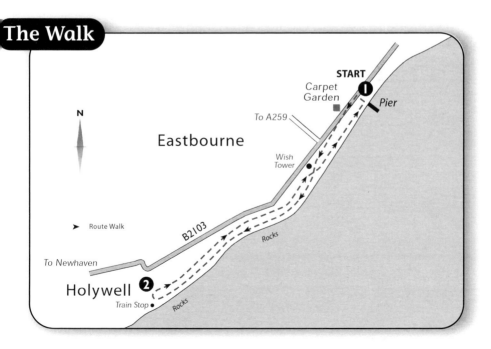

Kiddiwalks in East Sussex

1

❶ Start from the pier on Upper Parade and walk west past the Carpet Gardens and the Burlington Hotel. Swing left around the bandstand and right and continue past the Cavendish Hotel. Swing left downhill at the Eastbourne Lifeboat Museum and walk on past the Wish Tower Cafeteria on King Edward Parade to the Holywell Café.

❷ Turn right at the 'Train Stop' sign uphill and swing left at the

◆ Fun Things to See and Do ◆

Near the start of the route on the beach, is the departure point for **seasonal boat trips to Beachy Head**. One third of the way along the promenade is the **Eastbourne Lifeboat Museum** (free entry and open every day). It has a collection of models and a quiz for young people and a shop offering souvenir trinkets. Youngsters particularly enjoy rides on the **Dotto Train**.

The Dotto Train heads back to Eastbourne Pier

Holywell Drive sign. Turn right up Crows Nest Steps and continue straight forward on the gravel path. Take the right hand fork and go left at the Wish Tower Cafeteria, crossing the patio near the entrance. Turn right by the martello tower and go through the archway left. Weave right on the Lower Parade and go right and left by the bandstand, continuing back to the pier.

◆ Background Notes ◆

Eastbourne is a very attractive seaside town with a reputation for spruceness and gentility without the clamour of nearby Brighton. It has beautifully flowered seafront gardens but it lacks a sandy beach and its pebbles may not be attractive to some young children, although at low tide it has abundant rock pools and crevices for exploration. In pre-tourist days fishing boats once hauled up on the rocks – ask the children to find the remains of the little harbours. In Napoleonic times, several of the distinctively round, still-surviving martello towers were built locally to acknowledge the threat of invasion by the French.

One of the great sights of England is the arching cliffs just beyond Beachy Head known as the **Seven Sisters**. This spectacle may be enjoyed from the decks of a boat that operates during good weather in season from the temporary jetty near the pier.

The **Dotto Train** runs during the holiday period, the frequency of the service depending on demand. It is an electrically powered steam-lookalike traction engine that pulls carriages at a sedate pace along the promenade.

2
Alfriston
Meadow Sweet

The Cuckmere at Alfriston

The beautiful little village of Alfriston – one of the jewels of East Sussex and crowned by a church known as the Cathedral of the Downs – sits quietly beside a brook with pretensions. It calls itself a river but in the league table of watercourses, the delightfully named Cuckmere is in the stickleback division, although chub in the languorous pools and graceful swans on the surface create an instantly fascinating picture that may have peering children rooted to the first bridge! But onward MacDuff, to explore the nearby water meadows and to discover one of the tiniest churches in England.

This short walk between two bridges strikes out uphill on a leafy path that leads to the diminutive church of the Good Shepherd at Lullington Our route returns to Alfriston, circuiting its church and village green, known as the Tye. Such a picturesque setting draws artists from all over the south of England and children may wish to bring their own paints and brushes to join in the fun.

Getting there *The Cuckmere Valley is equidistant between Eastbourne and Newhaven. Alfriston is 1¹/₂ miles south of the A27.*

Length of walk 2 miles.
Time 2 hours, but allow a full morning for painting and picnicking and a full afternoon for enjoying the zoo.
Terrain Level riverside paths and one fairly steep field path ascent.
Start/Parking Park in the free (three hour duration) car park off West Street (GR 521033). If parking in excess of three hours, use the pay and display facility opposite. Toilet facilities are available close by.
Map OS Explorer 123 Eastbourne and Beachy Head.
Refreshments There are a number of dining options in Alfriston, three inviting pubs – the food in the George (telephone: 01323 870319) makes excellent use of local produce including fish and game in season and you have the choice of both bar and restaurant meals (it has an attractive garden for eating outside in summer) – and several good cafés, notably the Badgers Tea House on West Street (telephone: 01323 870849).

◆ Fun Things to See and Do ◆

The best spot for **painting** is over the White Bridge (see route description) on the left hand bank of the river opposite the church.

Set the children off on the path to the **hidden church next to Great Meadow Barn** (see route description) and see if they can discover it on their own ... they can't get lost!

Just down the lane going north towards the A27 is **Drusillas Park**, a splendid small zoo (see Walk 4 for details).

2

The Walk

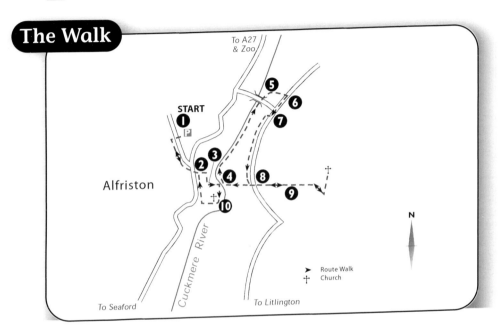

START P

To A27 & Zoo

Alfriston

Cuckmere River

To Seaford

To Litlington

N

➤ Route Walk
✝ Church

1 Leave the free car park by the vehicular entrance and go left on West Street to the High Street and the ancient village cross (*one of only two in the county*) in Waterloo Square.

2 Go left down River Lane to the banks of the Cuckmere.

3 Turn right to the White Bridge and cross left.

4 Turn left through the kissing gate and walk on the footpath

over the water meadows, heading upstream to the stone bridge. Go through the kissing gate.

5 Go right and turn immediately left through a kissing gate. Head diagonally right across a field to another kissing gate and go through to a quiet lane.

6 Turn right on the lane to an old trysting point at the junction marked by a walnut tree.

The scene near White Bridge

7 Cross the lane right at the bend and follow a public footpath sign marked 'South Downs Way' through a gate. Go left and follow the fence down, going through a gate to the bridge.

8 Turn left, cross the lane and go left and immediately right of Great Meadow Barn. You can unleash your offspring here with breathless shouts: 'Go right and left up the hill at the field edge, follow the path through the narrow wood and go left at the signpost to the church!'

9 Join the children and explore the old church then return to the bridge. Cross the bridge and the White Bridge and go left, following the river downstream.

10 Swing right towards the church through a gap in the fence and swing right opposite the Clergy House, skirting the Tye left to the 'Alfriston' sign. Go left up an alley, passing the Methodist church, and turn right on High Street to the cross and left back to the starting point.

2

◆ Background Notes ◆

A prosperous agricultural and market centre whose former importance is reflected in the size of its church, ancient **Alfriston** was given permission to hold a weekly market by Henry IV in 1405. This conservation village has many listed timber-framed houses and two old inns – the **Star** is one of the oldest in England and was originally a hostel owned by Battle Abbey. The wooden figure of a lion that guards its entrance was formerly the figurehead prow of a Dutch warship that was wrecked locally in the 1670s. Alfriston's proximity to the sea encouraged smuggling and the **Smugglers Inn** (its façade was recently demolished by a lorry and rebuilt) was the former home of Stanton Collins, leader of the Alfriston gang of smugglers. The inn was perfect for hiding contraband and for escaping from the clutches of excisemen. It has six staircases, twenty-one rooms and forty-seven doors!

The large church of **St Andrews** in Alfriston was founded in around 1360. Serving a largely pastoral community it had an endearing burial custom for shepherds. When one died, a tuft of wool was attached to his coffin to indicate to the Lord his genuine excuse for missing Divine Service during the lambing season. The practice died out in 1932.

The church of the **Good Shepherd at Lullington** dates from the 13th century, legend supposing that it was torched by Roundhead soldiers during the Civil War. What you see now are the remains of the old chancel. Inside the door on the left is a plan showing the building in its entirety. It seats 20 and is still used for worship.

3

Battle

Charge!

One date reverberates through English history like clashing swords. Even youngsters who are disinterested in the story of England can instantly recall the date of the Battle of Hastings. This compelling walk over the battlefield site, which has been preserved by English Heritage, uses a 'Prelude to Battle' exhibition, an introductory video and a series of interpretation boards and hand-held audio sets to explain the bloody events of that momentous day. There is an entrance fee for non-members of English Heritage but it is well worth it and children will enjoy using the simply operated audio equipment. A tour of the ruins of Battle Abbey can be included in your visit. Telephone 01424 773792 for opening times and charges.

The site of the battle of 1066 looking towards Battle Abbey

Kiddiwalks in East Sussex

3

Getting there *Battle is north of Bexhill and north-west of Hastings on the A2100.*

Length of walk 1¹/₂ miles.
Time The battlefield tour (with complete audio presentation) takes about an hour. Allow longer for exploring the abbey ruins and visits to the entrance shop.

Terrain Gently sloping formal paths, which are suitable for buggies.
Start/Parking Park in the pay and display car park on the west side of Battle Abbey (GR 748157). Toilet facilities are available close by.
Map OS Explorer 124 Hastings and Bexhill.
Refreshments There are numerous cafés and restaurants just a few hundred yards from Battle Abbey entrance.

The Walk

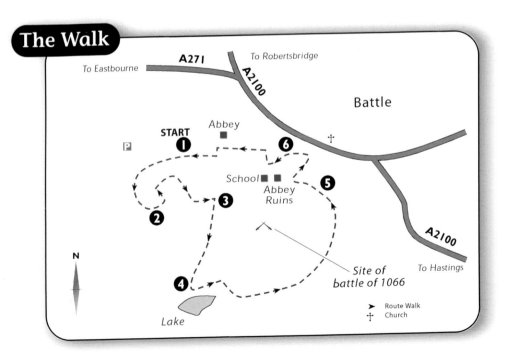

◆ Fun Things to See and Do ◆

Just to the left of Battle Abbey entrance is **Yesterday's World**. Its wonderfully crammed interiors – over 100,000 exhibits! – spirit us back to the bygone age of corner shops, sweets in jars, porcelain dolls, smiling assistants and a hairdresser's emporium that looks like a torture chamber. It comes complete with authentic sounds and smells, narration straight from grandma's knee, an audience with Queen Victoria, opportunities to enjoy old-fashioned slot machines, a 1930s railway station and a lovely garden and tea shop. It's a must for children! Open all year daily from 9.30 am. Telephone: 01424 775378. Battle has also a small museum of local history (back down the High Street from the Abbey – 250 yards on the left). Entry is free for children. Open April until October (closed Mondays).

❶ Go through Battle Abbey shop and collect an audio 'interpreter' (fee payable). Turn right from the shop and weave left to the 'Prelude to Battle' exhibition and the introductory video.

❷ Go left and right and stop to examine the model of Abbey and Battlefield. Continue left to the arrow markers.

❸ Go right through a gate following the yellow arrow marker and go through a second gate.

❹ Swing right and drop down left to a lake. Go through a third gate left and cross a footbridge and keep left. Swing left uphill to a gate.

❺ Go through right and make a loop left passing the old dairy, the ice house and the abbey basements (all open to view). Go right to the boundary wall.

❻ Go left to the entrance gate and the shop.

3 ◆◆◆◆◆◆◆◆◆◆◆◆◆◆◆◆◆◆◆◆◆◆◆◆◆◆◆◆◆◆

Yesterday's World

◆ Background Notes ◆

The **Battle of Hastings** was fought between Harold and William the Conqueror to decide who ruled England. The Norman knight landed at Pevensey Bay to the south and Harold marched from his stronghold in the North of England, having previously been victorious against his own brother Tostig at the Battle of Stamford Bridge (near York) the previous September. After an exhausting trek of some 400 miles, his men – many of whom were simple farmers – took on around 60,000 crack, professional French troops, electing to meet them at an eminence now occupied by Battle Abbey. The contest lasted all day and the outcome was in the balance until, by a ruse, William lured the Saxons from behind their palisades. Harold was killed as a shaft pierced him in the eye and the battle was lost. Traditionally he fell where an inscribed stone marks the site of the high altar of the abbey church built between 1070 and 1094.

4
Firle

Sussex Unfurled

Firle – the place of the mighty oak – sits cosily at the foot of the sweeping South Downs, rearing summits like Blackcap Hill, Heighton Hill and Gardner's Hill hiding it from the sea. An estate village, it nestles snugly under the twin wings of the mansion of Firle Place and St Peter's 12th century church, the absence of a through road allowing you to sniff the summertime roses and quaff a ginger beer at the Ram Inn in peace. But as you linger, you will be drawn to the beckoning tops, a magnificent view rewarding a climb to Firle Beacon. So drink up ... and off we go!

The longer version of this walk – energetic and exhilarating – is probably the most challenging for little legs in the book, rising to a height of 718 feet (217 metres), from where there is a 360 degree panoramic view of half the county. The shorter walk for younger children starts from a parking spot on top of the Downs offering the same breathtaking views without the climb.

Firle Beacon

Kiddiwalks in East Sussex

4

◆◆◆◆◆◆◆◆◆◆◆◆◆◆◆◆◆◆◆◆◆◆◆◆◆◆◆◆

Getting there *Firle is between Brighton and Eastbourne, around 5 miles south-east of Lewes and is easily accessed off the A27 Lewes to Eastbourne road.*

Length of walk $1^1/_2$ or $4^1/_2$ miles.
Time 1 hour or 4 hours.
Terrain Field edge tracks and parkland paths and (on the longer route) one steep ascent/descent to the Downs (not recommended for younger children).
Start/Parking Firle has thoughtfully provided its own free car park for visitors. It's on the left before you enter the village (GR 468074).
Map OS Explorer 123 Eastbourne and Beachy Head.
Refreshments The recently renovated Ram Inn in Firle offers a modern menu using locally sourced ingredients including fresh fish such as cod, bass and halibut. It has a pleasant seating area to the side. Telephone: 01273 858222. Alternatively, bring a picnic to enjoy one of the most spectacular outdoor feasts in the country. But who's carrying the bag?

◆ Fun Things to See and Do ◆

The ancient and exquisitely crafted brasses in **St Peter's church** (on the route) are probably the finest in Sussex and are well worth seeing. Here also are the recumbent 16th century alabaster effigies of Sir John Cage and his wife Lady Philippa Cage and the modern Piper Window installed in 1985 in memory of the sixth Viscount Gage. It depicts the Tree of Life, showing the Firle Oak and the famous breed of South Downland sheep.

Just east down the Eastbourne road (about 5 miles) is an award winning and quite innovative small zoo – **Drusillas Park**. It provides just the right mix of learning, adventure and play activities for young children. After his visit, 10-year-old Jamie from Berkshire said: 'Brilliant, cool, wicked. The rides are cool, the animals are cool. I've never seen anything like it.' Open every day. Telephone 01323 874100.

The Walk

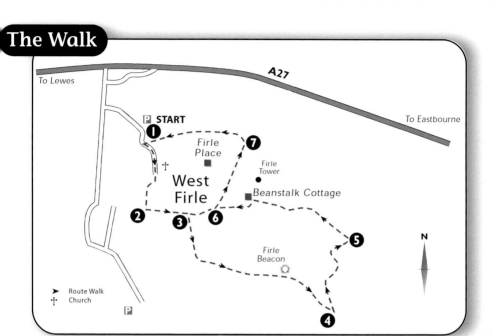

To Lewes

A27

To Eastbourne

P START ❶

Firle Place ■

❼

Firle Tower •

West Firle

† ■ Beanstalk Cottage

❷

❸

❻

❺

Firle Beacon ☼

N

➤ Route Walk
† Church

P

❹

---

❶ Go left from the car park through a side entrance and turn right on a track, going straight forward, following the sign along the lane to St Peter's church. Swinging right at the post office, go left down the path into the church grounds and visit the church. Walk straight forward from the porch and go right on the lane, following the public bridleway sign left at the forge.

❷ Go left, following the arrow marker, and ascend on a track to a copse of trees. (If you're opting for the shorter route, continue along the track for 200 yards and go left then follow the instructions from point 6.)

❸ For the longer route, turn right, following the arrow marker fieldside on an ascending track to the Downs, going through a gate and swinging left to the summit. After another gate, you reach Firle Beacon. Continue on the track right for about 700 yards.

Kiddiwalks in East Sussex

Do come and visit! (photo courtesy of Drusillas Park)

❹ Walk diagonally left to a gate and go through, continuing on a descending track to a further gate, going through and weaving right fieldside. Drop down through the edge of the trees to a track.

❺ Go left and continue, passing Firle Tower, to Beanstalk Cottage. Swing left and turn right along a shady track. At the next track right, go right.

❻ Continue until you reach an arrow marker into the grounds of Firle Place (permitted path) on the left.

❼ Go left and follow the line of arrow makers (at the top of posts), swinging left across the main access drive to a gate. Go through and walk on past the cottages to the post office, turning right back along the outward route to the starting point.

◆ Background Notes ◆

Firle Place is the ancestral home of the Gage family who have lived there for generations since the 15th century. Their imposing mansion was substantially improved around 1730, the family still owning large parts of the village and the pub! Thomas Gage introduced the greengage to England, first growing it at Firle Place. Another illustrious ancestor was the commander in chief of British forces in America at the outbreak of the American War of Independence. He fought and lost the opening salvo at Bunker Hill in 1775 and resigned his commission. Parts of Firle Place are open to the public but displays of pictures, French and English furniture and a famous collection of Sevres porcelain are not generally appreciated by children.

Sir John Gage and his wife are remembered in alabaster effigies in the church. This gentleman was a friend of Henry VIII and became the Constable of the Tower of London. Although he was a relative of the doomed Lady Jane Grey he had to preside over her incarceration and supervise her execution on the scaffold. The old king left Gage a sizeable legacy in his will.

The distinctive **Firle Tower** was built in the early 19th century as a gamekeeper's lookout from which he could survey the entire estate and signal orders to his beaters by flag-waving. It was once fitted with a telescope.

On the summit crest is a line of **ancient tumuli** where ancient chieftains were buried along with their prize possessions.

The triangulation pillar at **Firle Beacon** is now used by the OS as part of its global positioning system network.

If you want to cheat ... and I know you won't! ...you can drive to a parking spot on the top of the Downs (go back to the access road and turn left along Firle Bostal for just over a mile) and walk to the beacon from there.

5

Guestling Wood

Woodland Wonder

Springtime in Guestling Wood

This precious fragment of old England is every bit as valuable as the tropical rain forest. With only minor molestation it has survived for a thousand years or more, a swath of broadleaved trees arcing over carpets of spring bluebells offering a feast for the senses that cannot be enjoyed anywhere else in the world.

This wonderful winding ramble through woods awash with colour in every season leads to the millennium old church of St Laurence, the return route taking us past three ponds before another weaving woodland path takes us back to the start. Guestling Wood and the local hedgerows are home to many rare flowers and birds in season, including masses of bluebells, bugle, yellow archangel, centaury and foxglove together with nightingale and several species of warbler.

Guestling Wood

Getting there *Guestling Wood is around 2 miles south-east of Icklesham (A259) off a minor lane – Watermill Lane – immediately east of the Robin Hood pub. The lane is extremely narrow in places (few passing places, so be prepared to back up) but should be used to appreciate an example of an unimproved, classically English, hedged lane that is as equally splendid as the wood.*

Length of walk 2 miles.
Time 2 hours.
Terrain Gentle woodland and field paths.
Start/Parking Park in the car park provided by the Woodland Trust off Watermill Lane (GR 863145). Open between 8.30 am and 5.30 pm.
Map OS Explorer 124 Hastings and Bexhill.
Refreshments There are no refreshment facilities in the vicinity of this walk so bring a picnic and spread out your tablecloth at point 6.

The Walk

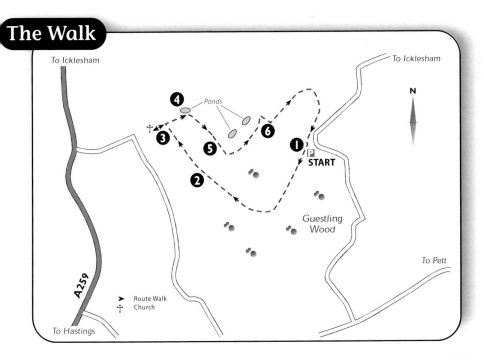

To Icklesham

To Icklesham

Ponds

④

③ ✝

⑤

⑥

❶
P
START

②

Guestling Wood

N

To Pett

A259

➤ Route Walk
✝ Church

To Hastings

Kiddiwalks in East Sussex

5

Starting them out young

❶ Go forward from the car park into the wood for 100 yards to the direction signs. Turn left on a path, following the yellow arrow marker. Drop down a slope and weave left and right uphill then take the right hand fork down to a bridge over a stream. Cross to a gap in the hedge at the perimeter of the wood.

❷ Leave the wood and take a distinctive path across a field up a rise to a distant hedged track to the right of the church.

❸ Go left on the track to visit the church then return along the track, keeping forward and going left downhill to a pond.

❹ Turn right along the wood edge and go right and left back towards Guestling Wood.

❺ Swing left past two ponds.

❻ Swing sharp right back into the wood and take the middle path, walking uphill and going left up the steps. Take the right fork and swing right back to the

◆ Fun Things to See and Do ◆

Other than nature at its wild best, there are no popular diversions to distract children from the pleasures of this outing. Bring field guides to identify the many **flowers and birds** you will encounter along the way. The track at point 3 positively bursts with blooms for many months of the year.

Guestling Wood

◆ Background Notes ◆

Guestling Wood is in the care of the Woodland Trust and extends to 25 acres. It was purchased in 1981 and a further 28 acres were added in 1987. The wood is mentioned in historical records going back to the Domesday Book. It is dominated by stands of sweet chestnut and oak together with birch, hazel and alder. On your walk you may see foxes and there are lots of rabbits.

Guestling church was one of the first built in Sussex by the Normans after the Conquest. It was destroyed by fire in 1886. By the time the horse-drawn fire engine arrived, it was a smouldering ruin. In the niche by the font is a statuette of St Laurence. He is shown holding a symbolic gridiron upon which he was martyred by the Romans in AD 258. Left of the altar is the fire-damaged monument to John Cheney, who died in 1603, and his wife Elizabeth. The carving originally showed a cradle and several kneeling children but these were lost to the flames.

6

Sheffield Park

Branches and a Branch Line

The Tower of London has the crown jewels but the National Trust's Sheffield Park has something far more precious, its national treasure of shrubs and trees out-sparkling any jewel. The shapes, the myriad different forms and leaves, the kaleidoscopes of colours that change with every season, the reflections in the lakes, the sumptuous blossoms and scents that simply drip from the branches in spring and summer ... all this will take your breath away!

This relaxing walk explores the park, using a network of intertwining footpaths and ornamental bridges over waterfalls and cascades. There is an entrance fee for non-members of the National Trust, telephone 01825 790231 for latest charges.

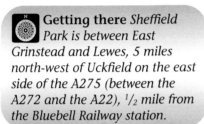

Getting there *Sheffield Park is between East Grinstead and Lewes, 5 miles north-west of Uckfield on the east side of the A275 (between the A272 and the A22), $^1/_2$ mile from the Bluebell Railway station.*

Length of walk $1^1/_2$ miles.
Time 2 hours.
Terrain Level formal footpaths suitable for all ages and for buggies (except the referred-to section of the woodland walk – point 9).

Start/Parking Park free in the signposted Sheffield Park car park (GR 413241). Toilet facilities are available in the gardens.
Map OS Explorer 135 Ashdown Forest.
Refreshments There is a formally laid out picnic site opposite the entrance to Sheffield Park. Near the entrance to the park is a tea room serving snacks and light lunches. Sheffield Park Station (Bluebell Line) has a cafeteria serving lunches and snacks.

◆ Fun Things to See and Do ◆

Children are really welcome at Sheffield Park. They are provided with interactive Tracker Packs and Tree Trail Guides and are encouraged to borrow palettes and art materials to make records of their visits. Afterwards, why not take a ride on the wonderful **Bluebell Railway** (just a $^1/_2$ mile down the road) and get smoke and steam in your nostrils and grit in you hair. Return steam-hauled trains run regularly between Sheffield Park, Kingscote and Horsted Keynes. In June each year the railway hosts Thomas the Tank Engine weekends. Both Thomas and Percy attend in 'puffson' together with Sir Topham Hatt (the Fat Controller), additional entertainment including Punch and Judy and magic shows, clowns and roundabouts. Advance tickets on 01825 720831. The railway also organises Santa Specials. Advance tickets on 01825 720806. You can buy a joint ticket giving family entrance to both Sheffield Park and the railway. Telephone: 01825 790231 or 01825 720800. Timetable telephone: 01825 720825.

The Walk

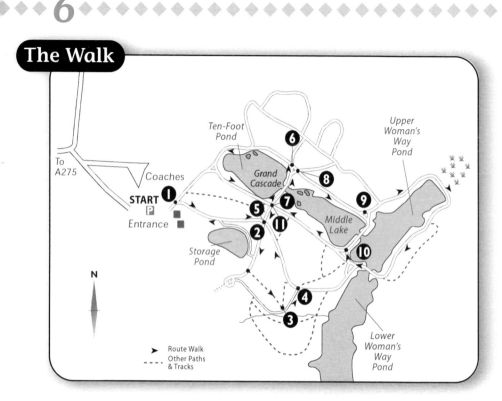

1 Fork right from the entrance shop and swing right.

2 Turn right and walk towards the work area. Go left off the main path down a minor path.

3 Swing left to the main path.

4 Turn left on the main path to the junction.

5 Turn right and continue over the intersection, crossing the Grand Cascade Bridge.

6 Turn left and arc around the Ten Foot Pond back to the intersection.

7 Re-cross the Grand Cascade Bridge left.

8 Turn right and continue, passing the Middle Lake and the magnificent sequoia tree on the left. Its relatives in the United States – they provided the seeds for Sheffield Park – are thousands of years old.

9 Fork left and make an almost complete circuit of Upper Woman's Way Pond, going right over Cascade Bridge and forking right back to the bank of Middle Lake.

10 Turn left on the main path to the intersection.

11 Turn left to the main crossing path, where you go right to return to the starting point.

The Bluebell Railway

Kiddiwalks in East Sussex

◆ Background Notes ◆

Sheffield Park, set in 100 glorious acres, is now divided into luxurious private apartments. In 1775, John Baker Holroyd, who later became the first Earl of Sheffield, commissioned Capability Brown to remodel his garden. The third Earl planted many of the exotic species we see today. Arthur Soames bought the property in 1909 and spent 25 years further enriching the gardens. The park is especially colourful in spring when its rhododendrons or rhodotentons (tell the children it's the heaviest plant in the world) and the azaleas bloom. The spring show is matched by the autumnal extravaganza when the glowing colours are magnified and mirrored in the lakes. The cricket-mad third Earl promoted the construction of the Bluebell Line and pioneered the concept of Test cricket in his grounds. In the long winter of 1890–1891 he arranged several cricket matches on the ice, coining the phrase: 'He's been caught in the slips.'

When the Lewes to East Grinstead railway was closed in 1958, a fervent band of steam enthusiasts stepped in to save the line. The **Bluebell Railway** was the first such volunteer-run enterprise to operate passenger trains. Starting with only two engines and a pair of carriages, the railway quickly expanded. Today it operates 30 locomotives and more than 100 carriages and wagons serving three fully restored stations that are often used by the movie industry for film making. The line attracts over 100,000 visitors each year. There are plans to extend the service to the mainline station in East Grinstead. For adults, the railway runs a Golden Arrow Pullman Service using refurbished vintage coaches, the VIP treatment including a gourmet meal en route. Telephone: 01825 720801.

Pooh Bridge

Get Your Bearings

You can dispense with a compass in finding one of the most delightful destinations in this book, a destination that, despite its minuscule size, draws as much attention as the some of the mightiest bridges in the world. Such is the magical power of the honey trail laid down by the author A.A. Milne and the attraction of his rotund little bear, Winnie the Pooh, that you could, along with children of many nationalities, walk this trail blindfolded.

The famous bridge is set in the midst of a mystical wood, the pitter patter of hundreds of little feet at all times of the year doing nothing to disturb the serenity of a wildlife haven strung with a network of paths.

Playing 'pooh sticks' at Pooh Bridge

This walk to the bridge and beyond takes you through one of the finest landscapes in Sussex, with long distance views of Ashdown Forest. The margins are resplendent with flowers in season and while bears with honey-sticky paws might be rather thin on the ground, if you are lucky like me, you will spy deer and squirrels.

Kiddiwalks in East Sussex

Getting there *Pooh Bridge is around 2 miles south-west of the village of Hartfield (between Forest Row and Groombridge) off the B2026 at Chuck Hatch. Turn off westwards and continue for 150 yards.*

Length of walk 2 miles.
Time 2 hours.
Terrain Gently undulating field and forest paths and two quiet country lanes, one with a fairly taxing short ascent to finish.
Start/Parking Park in the designated and free Pooh Bridge car park and begin the walk there (GR 473332).
Map OS Explorer 135 Ashdown Forest.

Refreshments There are no refreshment stops along the way. Around 3 miles south of Chuck Hatch alongside the B2026 at Duddleswell is the well-patronised Duddleswell Tea Rooms. It serves lunches and specialises in Pooh Bear Teas (including a free surprise gift for children) and Sussex cream teas. Open every day between June and August; closed on Mondays the rest of the year. Telephone: 01825 712126. In Hartfield to the north is the picturesque 14th-century Anchor Inn serving wholesome bar snacks and restaurant meals. Booking advisable, telephone: 01892 770424.

◆ Fun Things to See and Do ◆

In Hartfield on High Street is Pooh Corner, a shop devoted to the bear legend. Pooh's friend Christopher Robin was a regular visitor here when the premises served as the village shop. Open every day. Telephone: 01892 770424.
Website: www.pooh-country.co.uk

The Walk

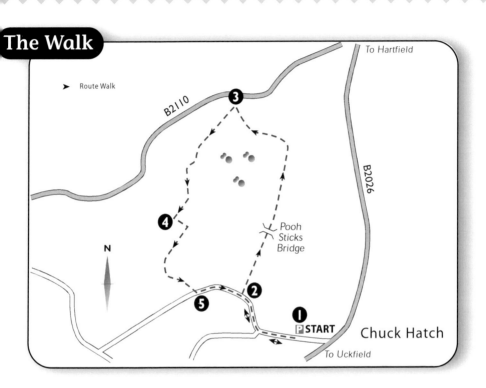

1 Turn left from the car park, following the direction sign to Pooh Bridge. Swing right and merge with the lane, passing the entrance gates to Andbell House. Continue for 60 yards.

2 Turn right on a track signposted to Pooh Bridge and drop downhill to the bridge. Walk forward on a track and pass the entrance to Ryecroft Farm on the left. Continue on the lane, forking left past Mole End and, ignoring the footpath sign on the right of the bend, walk up the lane left and pass The Chase and the drive to Little Cotchford on the left. Proceed for a further 100 yards.

3 Go left opposite the white stone, following the yellow arrow marker over a stile. Continue down alongside the hedge and go left over a stile in the field corner. Swing left and right, following the direction posts. Go left over the stile and walk across a meadow, crossing a further stile and going right to a stile by a pond.

4 Cross left to a track and go right at the entrance to Forest Springs. Drop down left by the hedge to a stile. Cross and veer left and right over the tussocky meadow and cross a footbridge in the corner over a stream. Swing left to the lane.

5 Turn left uphill and continue on the outward route back to the car park.

Water lilies can be seen on the pretty lakes

◆ Background Notes ◆

Born in 1882, **Alan Alexander Milne** moved to Cotchford Farm near Hartfield in 1925 and wrote his legendary books there. His first publication venture was a failure but he persevered, encouraged by the popularity of his children's verses. A journalist on *Punch* magazine he was inspired by his son Christopher Robin and his childhood toys, the landscape of Ashdown Forest creating the timeless backdrops for his cuddly heroes using local beauty spots such as Gills Lap Bridge (originally built for horses and carts) and the Five Hundred Acre Wood. Thousands of little feet wore out the original bridge of 1907 and it was replaced in 1979 and again in 1999 helped by a donation from publishers Methuen. Milne's books *The House at Pooh Corner* and *Toad of Toad Hall* have been translated into many languages and have created some of the most recognisable fictional characters in history. Milne died in 1956.

'I am a Bear of very Little Brain and long words bother me,' said Pooh.

8

Herstmonceux

An Ancient Castle, a Nine-Foot Ghost and a Rest-Home for Retired Daleks

Herstmonceux has had a certain Gallic charm ever since 1066, when the triumphant William the Conqueror raised his tattered standard at nearby Senlac Hill. For military services rendered, he conferred the local estates to one of his staunchest generals and there has been an imposing presence on the site ever since, the present moated pile, splendidly set among carefully maintained Elizabethan parklands and gardens, dating from the 15th century.

This charming and exciting walk begins in the shadow of a church that predates the castle by centuries. It leads on past the castle, whose tall ghost is said to beat a drum in a nightly tattoo on the battlements, through woodland margins and over meadows to the heart of an Observatory Science Centre, its copper topped domes looking like defunct escapees from the set of Doctor Who.

Herstmonceux Castle

Kiddiwalks in East Sussex

8

 Getting there *The start of the walk is nearly 2 miles south-east of Herstmonceux village down a dead-end road. Herstmonceux is around 3 miles north-east of Hailsham on the A271. From the eastern end of the village, turn off southwards (no signpost) on Chapel Row (leading to Church Road) and continue along the lane for about 1³/₄ miles until it stops near the church.*

Length of walk 2 miles.
Time 2 hours.
Terrain Gently undulating field paths and woodland margin tracks. Be prepared for some mud in wet weather.

Start/Parking Park on the verge outside All Saints'church (GR 643102).
Map OS Explorer 124 Hastings and Bexhill.
Refreshments Herstmonceux Castle has a tea room serving snacks and daily specials (telephone: 01323 833816). The Observatory Science Centre also has a tea room (telephone: 01323 832731). In Herstmonceux village is the Sundial Restaurant and Bistro (telephone: 01323 832217) – French inspired meals – and the Brewer's Arms (telephone: 01323 832226) – good bar snacks.

◆ Fun Things to See and Do ◆

Take a short detour at point 2 on the walk and go left into the grounds of **Herstmonceux Castle** and the **Observatory Science Centre**. The science centre is immediately right; the castle is further on down the drive.

The castle can only be visited as part of a guided tour available from Sunday to Friday. The grounds are open from April until October, attractions including flower gardens, a visitor centre, a nature trail, a children's woodland play area and a gift shop. Telephone: 01323 833816. Website: www.herstmonceux-castle.com

The science centre is the former home of the Greenwich Royal Observatory. Its astronomy-themed Discovery Centre has exhibits, daily science shows and telescope tours. Open daily (weekends only in January and December). Telephone: 01323 832731. Website: www.the-observatory.org

The Walk

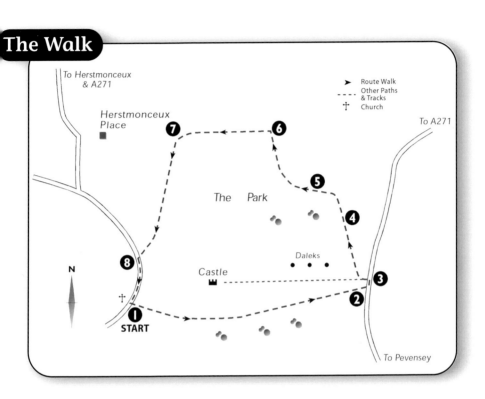

1 Go forward from the church for 60 yards and turn left to the gate. Go through and pass through a second gate to the right of the dome then go through a third gate left over a meadow, passing the castle to the left. Go through a fourth gate, following the bridleway sign, and climb up to a fifth gate opposite the domes. Keep going forward to the lane.

2 Walk to the left for 100 yards, passing the estate entrance.

3 Turn left, crossing a stile into woodland and following a footpath sign heading towards

Wild flowers abound in East Sussex

the domes. Veer right over the field to the corner.

4 Go left into the wood at the corner, following the arrow marker. Drop down by a fence line and cross a sleeper bridge over a ditch.

5 Bear left at the pole bench and weave left between two ponds, swinging right on a broad track. Continue forward, leaving the wood, to a gate.

6 Go left on a path over a field to the left of Herstmonceux Place.

7 Go through a gate left and swing right on a track (ignoring the footpath on the left). Continue to the lane.

8 Turn left along the lane back to the starting point.

◆ Background Notes ◆

Herstmonceux Castle was built in 1441 by Sir Rodger Fiennes in brick and became one of the great architectural spectacles of Sussex. One of Sir Rodger's descendants, Thomas, Lord Dacre, was executed on Tower Hill for the murder of a gamekeeper. The castle fell into a ruinous state and was abandoned in favour of Herstmonceux Place. Restoration took place beginning in 1912 by the castle's then owner, Colonel Claude Lowther, who raised battalions that became known as 'Lowther's Lambs' during the First World War. Lowther is commemorated in the church, a tablet recording that he found a ruin and left a palace. The building was requisitioned at the outbreak of the Second World War and then became the base for the Royal Greenwich Observatory. In 1993 it was bought by Dr Alfred Bader and given to his old university, Queens of Kingston, Ontario, Canada. It is now the Queens International Study Centre serving students from Canada and other countries.

The imposing **Herstmonceux Place** was built in 1778 on the site of a previous house. The property is now divided into flats.

All Saints' church has an interesting chapel, the exquisite Dacre Memorial Tomb of 1534 taking pride of place. The church has a spire that is covered, in the Sussex fashion, in cedar shingles. These are much loved by boring woodpeckers, which you can observe in the churchyard.

9

Crowhurst

Best Foot Fore Wood

The little village of Crowhurst rests serenely in a fold of the hills. Hardly a crow flight from the clamour of nearby Hastings, it is tranquillity itself, with its glorious old church, remains of a manor house and a venerably gnarled yew tree that may have been planted when King Harold was a lad combining to cast a timeless spell. Only the calls of pheasants (two notes with a violin bow on a rusty saw) and the music of the Powdermill Stream break the silence. That magnificent tree – I have a century old photograph before me showing it fitted with a door – is the theme for this walk to Fore Wood. An RSPB Nature Reserve, it resounds to birdsong and, in spring and summer, is simply bursting with wild flowers such as bluebells, yellow flags, red campions and foxgloves. The children may also discover owl pellets, badger footprints and herons fishing in the stream.

Our leisurely route describes a figure of eight, taking in the banks, which perfume the air and are massed by brown and steel-blue dragonflies in early summer.

Crowhurst's ancient yew may be 3,000 years old

Crowhurst

 Getting there *Crowhurst is around 2 miles north-west of the western outskirts of Hastings. Take Crowhurst Road off the B2092.*

Length of walk 2 miles.
Time 2 hours.
Terrain Gentle field and woodland paths with slight gradients.

Start/Parking Park on-street opposite the church or (preferably) on the lane opposite the church that leads to the railway station (GR 758123).
Map OS Explorer 124 Hastings and Bexhill.
Refreshments The Plough Inn is around ¹/₃ mile south of the church on Crowhurst Road. It serves popular bar meals. Telephone: 01424 830310.

◆ Fun Things to See and Do ◆

Inspect the **oldest living thing in East Sussex** to the left of the church porch. But don't get too close. Thousands of years old, she's a decrepit old thing!

In the village ¹/₂ mile south of the church on Crowhurst Road is a **children's recreation ground**. Crowhurst is famous for its annual Scarecrow Safari held on the first Saturday in June.

Hastings has a host of diversions for youngsters, not least its attractive beach and funfair. Based on the town's rugged past, the **Smugglers Adventure** re-lives the days of cut-throats and contraband, a web of exciting interactive displays in tunnels and caverns bringing the past alive. Nearby is the fascinating **Underwater World** aquarium, a long glass tunnel allowing you to 'walk beneath the waves' to observe a reef pool brimming with sharks, rays, crabs and starfish. Details respectively on 01424 422964 and 01424 718776.

The Walk

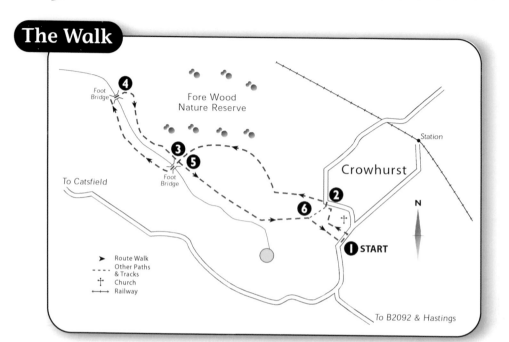

❶ Enter the churchyard and pass the great yew on the left, weaving right on the path at the back of the church to a gate. Go left along the lane to the bend.

❷ Go forward, following a signpost '1066 Bexhill Walk'. Keep forward at the corner and cross the field. Drop down between hedges left on a track and cross a second field, heading for Fore Wood. Cross a stile into the wood and drop down to a pond. Continue on a broad track uphill. Keep straight forward at

Map reading can be fun!

the marker post and at the log bench go left and left again to the footbridge over the Powdermill Stream.

3 Go over the footbridge and turn right, following the bank of the stream.

4 Turn right over the next footbridge and follow the direction marker right. Follow the next direction post marker left and drop downhill, returning to the log bench and swinging right to the first footbridge.

5 Turn left immediately before the footbridge and follow the east bank of the Powdermill Stream downstream. Go through a kissing gate and keep streamside, going through a second kissing gate left to a farm bridge.

6 Go left on a path and drop down to a gate. Continue through this towards the fragment wall of the old manor house. Go through a kissing gate to the lane and back to the starting point.

◆ Background Notes ◆

The **ancient yew tree** could be up to 3,000 years old. Legend has it that an uncooperative Saxon was hung from its branches just before the Battle of Hastings in 1066 for failing to divulge the whereabouts of Harold's army. After the Conquest, for services rendered, local lands in Crowhurst were given to the Earl of Brittany, although the Domesday Book records the area as devastated.

The **ruins adjacent to the church** are the only remains of a 13th century manor house raised by Walter de Scotney who was Chief Steward to the Earl of Gloucester. Scotney was tried and executed at Winchester for poisoning the earl and his brother.

The popular **Crowhurst Pumpkin Show** was initiated by former licencees of the Plough. The vegetables are judged in three classes – heaviest, best shaped and ugliest. In recent years there has been some cheating and pumpkins grown outside the parish have been banned.

10 Three Leg Cross

Backwaters

The duckpond at the Bull Inn

Three Leg Cross has become even more of a sleepy hamlet since the nearby reservoir of Bewl Water denied it a through road. It snoozes quietly on the southern shore of the largest lake in the south-east of England, a bankside exploration of its tranquil creeks and bays providing relaxation in wonderful scenery, with wildfowl and wild flowers of every description adding interest at every turn.

Getting there *Three Leg Cross is in the north-east of the county, east of Wadhurst near Ticehurst. Approaching from Wadhurst, take the B2099 and turn left just before Ticehurst village.*

Length of walk $2^1/_4$ or $3^1/_2$ miles.
Time 2 or 3 hours.
Terrain Easy shoreline footpaths and field tracks although the longer walk (point 6) uses a muddy track. After rain, it is not suitable for children under eight years old.

Start/Parking Park in the rear car park of the Bull Inn (if using the facilities) or on the nearby lane (GR 686311).
Map OS Explorer 136 High Weald.
Refreshments The 14th century Bull Inn in Three Leg Cross. Built between 1385 and 1425, this atmospheric pub serves bar and restaurant meals and specialises in steak dishes, roasts and home-made quiches. It has an inviting beer garden, a duck pond with a fountain, a dovecote, a children's play area and a petanque court. Telephone: 01580 200586.

Fun Things to See and Do ◆

Bewl Water is alive with birds – I saw swan, mallard, heron, grebe, coot, moorhen, cormorant, plover and tern – bring binoculars. The reservoir offers a host of activities for both adults and youngsters, including bike hire (telephone: 01892 891446), trout fishing (telephone: 01892 890352), sailing, canoeing and power boating (telephone: 01892 890716), windsurfing (telephone: 01892 891000) and lake cruises aboard the *Swallow* (telephone: 01892 890171). Bewl Water has its own restaurant (telephone: 01892 890171). To reach the Visitor Centre (parking fee payable) go back to Wadhurst and take the B2100 north-east towards Lamberhurst for 3 miles.

The Walk

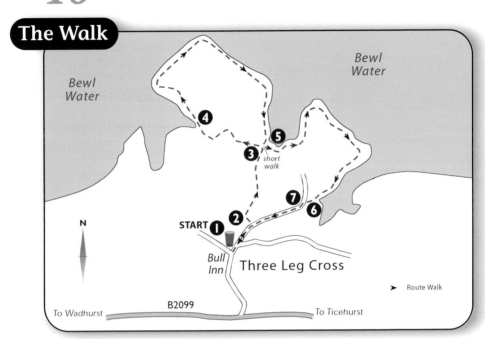

Bewl Water

Bewl Water

Bewl Water

4

5

3 *short walk*

7

6

N

START **1** **2**

Bull Inn

Three Leg Cross

➤ Route Walk

To Wadhurst

B2099

To Ticehurst

1 Go left from the inn along the quiet lane for 60 yards.

2 Go left again, following a footpath sign on the farm access road, and continue to the cattle grid and the Bewl Water signs.

3 Go left on a bridleway, swing right and go left to the shore.

4 Turn right on a footpath into the nature reserve at Grebe Corner. Swing right and pass the landing stage. Follow the path round to Dunsters Bay and continue to the marker posts.

5 *For the shorter walk, turn right here and make your way back to point 3, then go left, back on the outward route to the inn.*

For the longer walk keep forward. Swing left and follow the path and arrow markers round to Tinker's Marsh. Hidden in the trees to the right is Dunster's Mill House (see background notes).

Three Leg Cross

6 Just past an orchard on your right (near the water's end), look out for a footpath sign on your right. Turn right on the footpath uphill. Turn right after 150 yards to the lane.

7 Turn left on the lane back into Three Leg Cross.

Bewl Water

◆ Background Notes ◆

Three Leg Cross is a quieter alternative to the multiple activities offered at the **Bewl Water Visitor Centre**. Bewl Water is a valuable recreational and wildlife environment and is home to well over 2,000 different plants, animals, insects and bird species including Brent geese and white-fronted geese. Part of it is managed in conjunction with the Sussex Wildlife Trust, some of our route – point 4 – passing through their reserve. The reservoir was built between 1973 and 1975 by damming a tributary of the Medway River. It covers 770 acres and holds some 6,900 million gallons of water to a depth of over 60 feet. When plans for the reservoir were being advanced, it became obvious that the Dunster Watermill (see point 5 of the walk) would be submerged. The outraged owner petitioned Parliament to complain and Southern Water were obliged to dismantle the property brick-by-brick and resurrect it in its present position away from the shoreline.

11
Rye

Tripping Along the Cobbles

The River Tillingham

This fairytale little town rises above the lush marshes, its old defensive walls and gates, cannon and look-out towers harking back to prosperous days when trade was good and everybody had to be tucked up in bed before the portcullis was dropped shut. One of the Cinque Ports, Rye grew rich before its local watercourses silted up and the sea retreated. The port blossomed from the profits of trade, the modern town presenting a delightful assemblage of picturesque old red-shingled houses, cobbled streets and quiet car-free precincts bright with gardens and window boxes.

This tour treads a labyrinthine way down the most interesting streets, offering places to explore almost on every corner.

Getting there *Rye is between Hastings and New Romney on the A259.*

Length of walk 2¹/₄ miles.
Time 2 hours.
Terrain Some steep streets and the cobbles can be a tripping hazard for young feet in places.
Start/Parking Start on the eastern side of the town and park in the Bedford Place pay and display car park (GR 923206). Toilet facilities are available close by.
Map OS Explorer 125 Romney Marsh, Rye and Winchelsea.

Refreshments There are numerous cafés and restaurants in Rye.

❶ Turn right from the car park to the roundabout and go left, then swing left up Landgate under the old gateway. Continue along Hilder's Cliff to the lookout point. The view south is over Romney Marsh to the tree-clad heights of Iden. Swing right.

❷ Turn right down the cobbled Conduit Hill to the roundabout.

❸ Turn left on Cinque Ports Street.

◆ Fun Things to See and Do ◆

The **Rye Town Model Exhibition** is located at point 8 on the route. Seven hundred years of local history are brought to life in this dramatic exposition, with narration and sound and light effects combining brilliantly to show how the town developed. On the upper floor is a collection of old slot machines and coin-in-the-slot mechanical tableaux. Open daily from Easter until November. Telephone: 01797 223902.

The **Gun Garden** is located in point 10 on the route. Children will revel in a hands-on experience of pretending to repel invaders using the black cannon.

The Walk

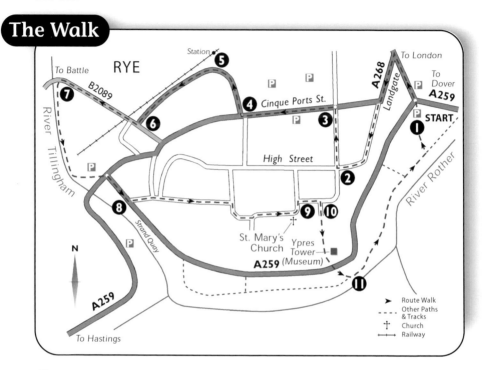

4 Turn right on Station Approach.

5 Turn left on Crown Fields and continue beside the railway line to Ferry Road.

6 Turn right down Ferry Road and go over the level crossing to Rye Pottery on your right beside the River Tillingham.

7 Turn left on a riverside footpath and pass the windmill. The original structure was destroyed by fire in 1930 and rebuilt. Cross the railway line and continue to the road, weaving left and right to the Strand Quay.

8 Turn left by the Rye Town Model Exhibition and continue up the cobbled Mermaid Street, swinging right on West Street to reach St Mary's church. Continue to the church front entrance.

9 Turn left on Lion Street and go immediately right on Market Street.

10 Turn right on Pump Street past the old Water Tower and proceed to the Ypres Tower Museum (selective opening – telephone: 01797 226728). Descend the steps in front of the Gun Garden and cross the A259, going straight forward on Rock Channel.

The Old Ferry Cottage

⓫ Go left along the raised footway near the old Ferry Cottage. *Until 1927 this was the home of the local ferryman. Dryshod shepherds would bring their flocks to market in Rye. But sheepdogs were charged at full fare and had to swim alongside the flocks.* Go left off the bank back to the car park.

◆ Background Notes ◆

Rye was one of the **Cinque Ports** charged with helping defend the Channel coast against French invasion, its status bringing trading privileges. In the 16th century, the sea retreated leaving only constricted and shallow access along the local river courses. The harbour is now two miles downstream. The **Water Tower** (point 10) was built in 1735 to provide the town's water supply. It was used for the dumping of rubbish and rewards were offered for information leading to the arrest of miscreants responsible for disposing of trash like calves' feet! The **Ypres Tower** dates from the 13th century. It was supposed to deter the French although it fell to their depredations in 1377 when they entered the town and burnt every one of its wooden buildings. The cannon in front of the tower were manufactured in 1980 to commemorate the 80th birthday of Queen Elizabeth the Queen Mother, Lord Warden of the Cinque Ports. They replaced a battery of six brass pieces impressed with the arms of Spain. These were presented to the town by Elizabeth I in recognition of the part Rye played in the defeat of the Armada.

12
Salehurst

Hop It!

An oast house conversion

The small and timeless village of Salehurst is the starting point for an exhilarating and scenic walk through countryside that was once dominated by hop gardens, fields festooned with poles and oast houses at every hedge corner, giving a certain nasal air to the local landscape. Nearly all the oast houses have been converted to residential use – planning restrictions have thankfully led to the preservation of the distinctive conical roofs – and most of the gardens lie fallow although one survives in all its hoppy glory near to the start of our ramble. There is something uniquely English about the landscape in this area that makes you want to fly the flag of St George from your knapsack!

The route passes over the River Rother and by a large lake adjacent to Salehurst Farm. It continues through the fringes of Wellhead Wood – this abounds with bluebells in springtime – and past the ruins of Robertsbridge Abbey.

Getting there *Salehurst is on a minor road near Robertsbridge off the A21 to the north of Battle. Turn off eastwards at the Northbridge Street roundabout and continue on Church Road for just under a mile.*

Length of walk $2\frac{1}{2}$ miles.
Time 2 hours.
Terrain Easy quiet lanes, farm tracks and footpaths.
Start/Parking Park around the big tree to the right of St Mary the Virgin church in Salehurst (GR 749243).
Map OS Explorer 136 High Weald.
Refreshments Near the start of the walk is the inviting Salehurst Halt pub, which has a lovely country garden. It offers good bar and restaurant meals using local produce and fresh-caught fish such as cod and monkfish. There is a children's menu. Telephone: 01580 880620.

◆ Fun Things to See and Do ◆

Nearby in Robertsbridge is the **Rother Valley Steam Railway** opposite the mainline station. It's currently being developed by volunteers to provide the 'missing link' between Robertsbridge and the Kent and Sussex Railway at Bodiam. The railway operates a locomotive on the site but is not able at present to provide passenger rides although visitors are welcome. Telephone: 01580 881833.

The **Kent and East Sussex Railway** operates a $10\frac{1}{2}$ mile line between Tenterden Town and Bodiam calling at Northiam, offering up to five steam-hauled services every day. Telephone: 0870 6006074. Talking Timetable: 01580 762943. Go north from the Northbridge Street roundabout and turn first right through Silver Hill to the crossroads. Go straight over for a further $1\frac{1}{2}$ miles to Bodiam.

Bodiam Castle is a fairy tale moated fortress built in 1385. It has lots of exhibits and a year-long programme of family events. Telephone: 01580 830436.

The Walk

1 Walk south away from the parking area by the side of the church and go left on a path, weaving right to Church Bridge over the River Rother. Cross to the lane.

2 Go right to the first oast house, passing a hop garden on the right.

3 Turn left down the access drive to Salehurst Park Farm.

4 Swing right and left by the farm.

5 Swing right again and go left, following the bridleway sign, on a track. Go through a gate and walk straight forward to the edge of Wellhead Wood. Go through a second gate and continue along the woodland edge.

6 Swing left and go forward, merging with a hard track.

7 Go left at the bridleway sign and go right to the lane.

8 Go left and right at the corner, passing Robertsbridge Abbey.

9 Swing left and continue to the outward route.

10 Turn right over Church Bridge back to the starting point.

Entrance to St Mary the Virgin church. The Salamander Font can be seen through the doorway on the left

Background Notes ◆

Ancient **Salehurst**, meaning the place of the willows in dense woodland, is world famous together with nearby Robertsbridge as the home of cricket bat making. The 800-year-old church has one treasure that will fascinate children. Its **Salamander Font** near the doorway was, by tradition, presented by Richard the Lionheart as a reward to the abbot of **Robertsbridge Abbey** for helping secure his release from captivity in Bavaria. The abbot led an expedition to search for the king and secured his freedom with a ransom of 150,000 marks. The salamander was the emblem of the crusaders. The abbey was founded about 1176 and there is some evidence to suppose that it was moved to its later position where the ruins can still be seen. What was the abbot's house is now a private residence.

13

Barcombe and the Ouse

Messing About on the River

Fresh from the sea, salmon and sea-trout have ascended the sparkling River Ouse for centuries, this exciting depth-peering walk following their tails upstream over one of the oldest toll bridges in the country, past the site of once-busy mills and on over water meadows to the famous Anchor Inn.

Children will enjoy bankside paths alive with rabbits, voles, squirrels, insects, flowers and birds of every kind, including the fabulous kingfisher – several river crossings, as narrow and as adventurous as rope-bridges (but less precarious!), providing extra thrills. Young anglers are well catered for, many accessible glides and pools holding sizeable shoals of coarse fish, and should the family want to take to the water, boats are available for hire at the halfway stage. And a grand finale to a memorable day could be a ride on a steam engine.

The Ouse is full of wildlife

Barcombe and the Ouse

 Getting there *The starting point is accessed off a minor road 3 miles north-east of Lewes off the A26 Uckfield road. Turn westwards almost opposite Clayhill Nurseries and proceed for about ³/₄ mile to the signposted parking area.*

Length of walk 2¹/₂ miles.
Time With plenty of time for lingering and paddling on the river, allow at least 4 hours for this outing or a whole day if intending to take a rail trip.
Terrain Gentle field paths and riverbanks.

Start/Parking The walk begins in the designated and signposted Barcombe Mills car park alongside the river opposite Bridge Farm (GR 435146).
Map OS Explorer 123 Eastbourne and Beachy Head.
Refreshments There are numerous beautiful picnic spots along the riverbank and, at the halfway stage, the inviting Anchor Inn. It has a popular patio area overlooking the boat-hire jetty and offers a special children's menu and a wide range of choices for adults, including oven-baked trout, shoulder of lamb and vegetarian options. Telephone: 01273 401029.

◆ Fun Things to See and Do ◆

This **exceptional stretch of the River Ouse** is ideal for introducing young people to the delights of angling. Bird life is also prolific along the margins (enjoy the resident swans and Canada geese and notice the boxes provided for tawny and barn owls) and young ornithologists should be encouraged by providing binoculars. The highlights of the day though should be either (or both!) a **boat trip from the Anchor Inn**, upstream on a leisurely cruise of two or more hours, or a ride on the **Lavender Line** steam railway.

The Walk

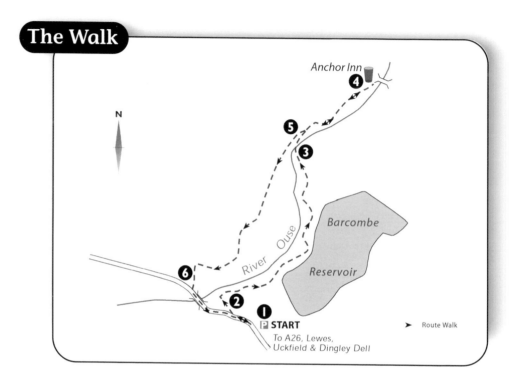

❶ Turn left from the car park towards the big oak tree. Swing left towards the lane and then right over Pike's Bridge.

❷ Turn right before you get to the second bridge, following the public footpath sign on a path and going through the kissing gate by the pillbox. Go left over the footbridge by the fishing sign and follow the yellow arrow marker right along the bank. Pass through a kissing gate by the

pumping station and swing left, going left at the Slaugham Angling Club sign over a second footbridge, swinging right, going through a kissing gate and following the arrow marker along the bank to a field access bridge.

❸ Turn left over the bridge and go immediately right on the lane towards the old mill house and the millstones. Follow the footpath sign left and swing right to the pillbox and follow the

Technology on the Lavender Line

riverbank up, going through a kissing gate to the car park of the Anchor Inn.

4 Retrace your steps to the field access bridge.

5 Keep going straight forward here and cross a bridge, swinging right towards the houses.

6 Go next left between the houses, crossing a bridge over the river and re-cross Pike's Bridge back to the starting point.

Kiddiwalks in East Sussex

13

◆ Background Notes ◆

This tidal stretch of the **Ouse** was once an important commercial artery, horse-drawn barges travelling up the river from Newhaven to Slaugham with various cargoes, which included bricks, used to build the Barcombe Railway Viaduct in 1861. **Mills** existed at Barcombe from before the time of Domesday, producing a variety of agricultural products and, in more recent times, buttons. The last mill was burnt to the ground in 1939.

There are many historical structures along the route of this walk. The most recent is the **Second World War pillbox**, one of many that were intended as a second line of defence in the event of an invasion by the Germans.

Children will be particularly fascinated by the **salmon ladders** (see walk description, points 3 and 6) installed in mid-flow to assist fish in their annual migrations to the spawning beds (the redds) in the upper reaches.

Youngsters under 14 years of age are exempt from the need to buy annual fishing rod licences although they will need day tickets (see local sign boards for information). Boats for 2, 4 or 6 people are available for hire at the Anchor Inn kiosk during the summer months (credit cards only – no cash). Children under 14 years of age are required to wear life jackets (provided).

To complete a memorable outing, steam-train rides on the nearby **Lavender Line** at Isfield (3 miles) are available on Saturdays, Sundays and Bank Holidays with special Santa excursions arranged during the Christmas period (drive back to the Clayhill Nurseries turn and go left on the A26, forking next left to the Dingley Dell Terminal). Timetable information: 01825 750515. Children's parties can be arranged in an original British Railways carriage. Telephone: 01444 831687. The railway was part of the Lewes–Uckfield line, which closed in 1969.

14
Arlington

Des Res

Fly-fishing on Arlington Resevoir

Arlington Reservoir was formed by intercepting the waters of the delectable Cuckmere River and is set like a jewel in a beautiful landscape overlooked by the Wilmington Giant, an ancient figure of a man etched into the chalk of distant downland. The encatchment has created a notable nature reserve, the finest accolade of its achievement coming in the regular appearance of ospreys, which head an impressive visitors and residents list that extends to some one hundred and seventy three species. The reserve is also home to twenty-one types of butterfly, myriads of wild flowers, prodigious numbers of rainbow trout, bream, roach and eels and lots of little bunnies!

This easy walk circles the reservoir along a route designated as the Osprey Trail, the path darting off to explore a quiet reach of the Cuckmere under the tranquil gaze of the spire of the church of St Pancras in Arlington where you can stop for lunch in the village pub.

Kiddiwalks in East Sussex

14

Getting there *Arlington Reservoir is north-west of Eastbourne off the A27 Lewes road. Drive north from the Drusillas roundabout to Berwick Station for just under 2 miles and go over the level crossing.*

Length of walk $2^3/_4$ miles.
Time 3 hours.
Terrain Flat and easy (although it can be muddy in wet weather) and suitable, for the most part, for buggies with good suspension, although the diversion to Arlington village is not recommended.

Start/Parking Park in the Arlington Local Nature Reserve pay and display car park off the Berwick station/Upper Dicker road, the B2108 (GR 527075). NB: the car park closes at 8 pm. Toilet facilities are available close by.
Map OS Explorer 123 Eastbourne and Beachy Head.
Refreshments The nature reserve is provided with picnic tables. The Yew Tree in Arlington has a good range of bar meals, its menu including local meats and game such as wild boar in season. Telephone: 01323 870590.

The Walk

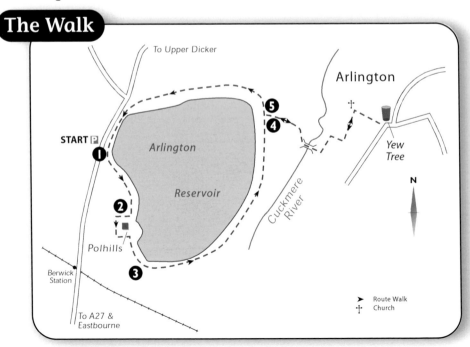

Arlington

1 Walk to the shoreline and turn right past the fishing lodge, continuing to the drive of Polhills Farm.

2 Swing right across the driveway and go left in an arc round the farmhouse, going right for 100 yards to a signpost.

3 Go left through a gate onto the dam wall and walk on in an arc left to a gate. To the south are good views of the Wilmington Giant.

Arlington Reservoir

4 Leave the Osprey Trail and go right over a stile, following a footpath sign to Arlington village and heading for the church spire. Cross the stile onto the Cuckmere River footbridge, go over a second stile and veer left, crossing a third stile. Continue hedgeside to the next direction marker and cross a footbridge over a ditch left,

continuing over a meadow left towards the church. Go through a kissing gate into the church grounds and turn right on a path to the lychgate. Continue on the lane to the Yew Tree. Return to the end of point 3.

5 Turn right and pass the track to the bird hide on the left and walk on, arcing left back to the starting point.

◆ Fun Things to See and Do ◆

Trout fishing can be enjoyed (fly only) from the bank or from boats. Telephone: 01323 870810 for details.

Arlington has its own **bird hide** located on the route of the Osprey Trail (point 5) and many rare birds can be seen from its windows although binoculars are recommended.

Kiddiwalks in East Sussex

14

Completed in 1971, **Arlington** is designated as a Site of Special Scientific Interest by English Nature. It covers 49 hectares – the size of 121 football pitches – has a maximum depth of 11.3 metres and a capacity of 3,500 million litres of water equivalent to the contents of 11,665 million cans of coke! It serves the Eastbourne, Polegate, Hailsham and Heathfield areas. During the excavation works remains were found of mammoth, bison and woolly rhinoceros.

Full explanatory details of the **Osprey Trail** are given in a leaflet. Copies of these are provided free of charge. Pick one up from the boxes located at the start of the walk.

The **Wilmington Giant** is one of the most instantly recognisable sights in Sussex and one of the largest representations of the human form in the world. Cut into the chalk of the Downs – 230 feet high with twin staves in his hands – he has existed since time immemorial. He was probably created as a fertility symbol or as an object of veneration. His outline was once delineated in yellow bricks but these were replaced by whitewashed concrete blocks in 1873. Seen from close quarters, he appears to be abnormally tall but from a distance he is perfectly proportioned, suggesting that his creators had a good knowledge of perspective. Rudyard Kipling wrote a poem in his honour:

> *I will go out against the sun*
> *Where the rolled scarp retires,*
> *And the Long Man of Wilmington*
> *Looks naked towards the shires …*

The **church of St Pancras** in Arlington village incorporates Roman brickwork – the imperial highway passed close by. Near the church and reputedly connected with it via an underground tunnel is the 14th-century **Woodhorne Manor**, a previous haunt of a desperate gang of smugglers. In recent times, the house has been plagued by the ghostly cries of drunken and argumentative men and the sounds of raucous parties are heard even when the place is empty.

15
Horam

Smoke, Steam and Iron

Friends encountered along the way.

These symbols of the Industrial Revolution dominated the local landscape for decades, charcoal burning, iron smelting and the arrival of the railways in the middle of the 19th century leaving a legacy of coppiced woodland, abandoned pits and silent trackways. Over a century on, with a wave of her green wand, Old Mother Nature has wrought a leafy transformation – profusions of trees and wild flowers, abundant wildlife, ponds full of fish and former railway cuttings echoing only to the swish of bicycle wheels – creating one of the most attractive destinations for rambling in East Sussex.

This walk of contrasts uses part of the 13-mile-long Cuckoo Trail, a pedestrian and bicycle way on the route of a former railway line. Part of our circuit traverses a farm certified by the Soil Association (see colourful accreditations on gates) as suitable for the production of organic food, the enthusiasm of the farmer for sustainable husbandry and for the protection and encouragement of wildlife … and walkers! … being wonderfully demonstrated in the development of hedges, ponds and footpaths. Children might like to be introduced to the notions of organic farming as they walk along.

Kiddiwalks in East Sussex

15

Length of walk $2^3/_4$ miles.
Time $2^1/_2$ hours.
Terrain One short hill climb, otherwise flat and level using an abandoned railway line, quiet lanes and field paths. But there are a lot of stiles to negotiate … at least 15!
Start/Parking Park in Horam village in the free car park off Hillside Drive (GR 577175), 250 yards north-east of the A267/B2203 junction. Toilet facilities are available close by.
Map OS Explorer 123 Eastbourne and Beachy Head.

Refreshments Horam has a number of dining options, including the Trawlerman Fish and Chip Shop, the Baker Café and the Home Farm Café.

❶ Turn right and go immediately left, following the sign to the Cuckoo Trail. Go left, following the signpost to Heathfield on the Cuckoo Trail. Cross Hendalls Farm Bridge and leave the old track at the next exit.

❷ Turn right on a lane and cross the junction, continuing straight forward down the opposite lane for 150 yards.

◆ Fun Things to See and Do ◆

Horam Home Farm – signposted access immediately left of the village as you approach from the south – has a number of attractions for children, including a nature trail and a small museum displaying artefacts from grandma's era. The exhibits include hop stilts – see Walk 11, the Salehurst route. And what were the farm's iron ore pits now provide a series of fishing ponds. Low-cost day tickets are available. Telephone: 01435 812955.

The Walk

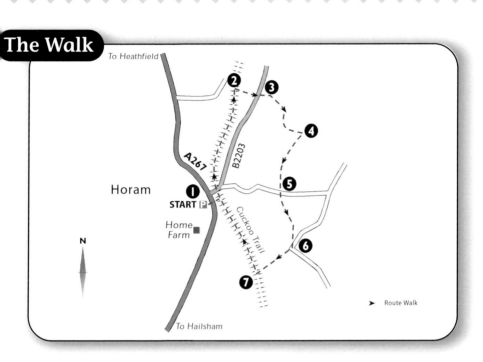

❸ Go right, following a footpath sign over a stile (organic farm) and heading left over a field for the corner. Cross a stile and swing right through a gate into a wood. *Look very carefully and you will discover several mounds and rust-stained pools showing that this area was once used for iron ore extraction.* Cross a bridge over a stream through the bluebell wood and go straight on over a single-planked bridge past a pool to the left. Leave the wood and bear left, following the arrow marker by the stile. Keep to the wood edge, cross the plank over the ditch and cross

Fisher lads at Home Farm.

the stile then go right, heading across the field to the hedge.

4 Do not cross the stile but turn right, following the footpath sign. Cross a stile between two wildlife ponds. Continue forward at the bend, following the arrow marker over a stile. Go through a copse and cross the next stile, following a footpath marker into the vineyard estate, and continue going forward by the picnic tables, crossing a stile to the lane.

5 Go over the lane, turn left for 5 yards and then right, following a public footpath sign. Cross a stile, following an arrow marker left over a footbridge, and veer right uphill. Cross a stile left to the field corner. Go over another stile and walk straight across a meadow to a stile which brings you onto Laundry Lane.

6 Cross the stile by Willow Cottage, continue forward and go over a stile and a footbridge, crossing a further stile, going left and over a stile to the Cuckoo Trail.

7 Turn right along the Cuckoo Trail for $^3/_4$ mile and make your way back to the start.

◆ Background Notes ◆

Horam was a sleepy place until the coming of the railway, the sprawling modern village occupying a convenient location at the junction of the A267 and the B2203. It has been the home of Merrydown Cider since 1946; the firm is still operating in the village and providing employment for local people.

This walk passes through a vineyard, the area around Horam developing a growing reputation for fine wines. Just to the north-west is **St George's Vineyard at Waldron**, its vintages attracting international interest from as far away as Japan.

The railway serving the High Weald, the Cuckmere Valley and the area around the Pevensey Levels was built by the London Brighton and South Coast Railway Company in 1849. To obtain a free **Cuckoo Trail** leaflet contact 01323 442667.

16
Exceat

A Stroll in the Park

Cuckmere Haven and the Seven Sisters.

Exceat was once a sleepy hamlet consisting solely of isolated farmsteads near Cuckmere Haven alongside the towering Seven Sisters cliffs. Since 1977 it has been the operational centre for the 700-acre Seven Sisters Country Park, thousands of people every year coming to enjoy one of the last undeveloped river estuaries in Southern England. Walkers, cyclists and canoeists throng here in the summer season but the wide open spaces accommodate them all. It is still easy to find peace and solitude alongside the Cuckmere River whose lazy, serpentine meanders put me in mind of my old granddad's pipe smoke as he snoozed by the fire. This exhilarating ramble initially climbs the green heights on the South Downs Way giving spectacular views of the river before dropping down to a wonderful shingle beach beneath the chalk cliffs. The return route is on a hard path at the water's edge.

Kiddiwalks in East Sussex

16

 Getting there *Exceat is between Eastbourne and Seaford on the A259.*

Length of walk 3 miles.
Time 3 hours.
Terrain One steep upward climb on downland turf, an uneven pebbly beach and a flat-concreted path on the return.
Start/Parking Park in either of the two pay and display car parks near the Visitor Centre (GR 518995). Toilet facilities are available close by.
Map OS Explorer 123 Eastbourne and Beachy Head.
Refreshments Exceat Farmhouse next to the Visitor Centre. Snacks and restaurant meals – cream teas a speciality. Telephone: 01323 870218.

◆ Fun Things to See and Do ◆

 In the **Visitor Centre** are touchy/feely displays and quizzes for children, giving insights into local geology, river systems and wildlife. Centre rangers post details of daily sightings of birds such as dunlin, whitethroat, black winged stilt, godwit and avocet, with reports also covering wild flowers and rare plants. Printed trail guides are available describing interesting sights and objects along the way. Next to the Visitor Centre is a bicycle hire shop – **The Cuckmere Cycle Company** – with a range of bikes for adults and children. Their fleet includes tandems and rickshaw type vehicles with little seats at the back for toddlers! The shop also provides local route guides to the hamlet of West Dean and the extensive tracks through Friston Forest. Free of cars, you can access West Dean and the forest direct without travelling on public roads.

The Walk

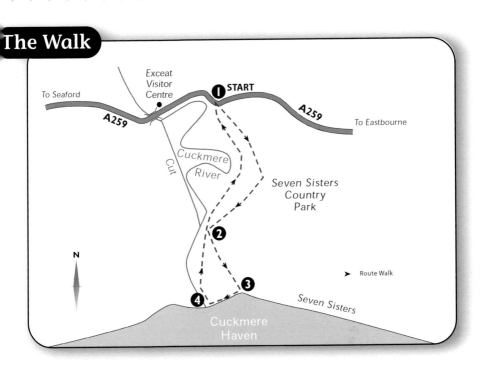

1 Cross the road opposite the Visitor Centre and go left of the bus pull-in to a gate. Go through and go left, following the yellow South Downs Way sign uphill on a grassy track. Where the track divides at the marker post, swing right and go through a kissing gate, heading downhill towards the Haven and to the right of a rectangular pond. Go through a gate at the bottom.

2 Turn left to the gate and go through, walking on to the next direction post. Go left, following the yellow South Downs Way sign, and then swing right at the bottom of the hill, following the sign to the beach.

3 Turn right over the shingle beach to the Cuckmere Haven sign and the river outlet.

4 Turn right on a track. Go through a gate and walk on to the next gate. Go through and follow the concrete path left to the road and the starting point.

The Seven Sisters

◆ Background Notes ◆

Exceat is one of the lost villages of Sussex mentioned in the Domesday Book but by 1460 it consisted of just two houses and a ruined church. Frequent raids by French pirates were the most likely cause of depopulation and abandonment, although the visitation of the Black Death was a likely contributory factor.

Cuckmere Haven and the **Cuckmere River** have been used by commercial vessels over the centuries – part of the channel was straightened – but the unpredictable nature of winds and tides and the constantly changing shape of the shingle bank have made the landing a precarious one. But it was a convenient spot for smuggling! This precious resource is being allowed over the next couple of decades (with a little help) to revert to its natural form to optimise wildlife and to create an exceptional habitat particularly for birds and flowers. At low tide, you can feast your eyes on the luscious dazzling white curves of the **Seven Sisters** cliffs to the east.

As you walk around the park you will notice one isolated and several clusters of **Second World War pillboxes** located at strategic positions to defend the beach in the event of invasion by German forces. The blocks to the left of the gate at point 4 on the walk are tank traps and they are in their original position.

17

Fairlight

Sights for Soar Eyes

T he portal to an extensive coastal country park, the village of Fairlight keeps a constant vigil above the sea, its coastguard station and lighthouse-like tower of St Andrew's church surveying a stretch of eroded cliffs that are disappearing at the rate of 145 yards or so every one hundred years. At the end of the millennium, most of the Hastings County Park will be gone. It's a magnificent windswept place of rolling hills and leafy dells and breathtaking views, a diverse geology creating a variety of habitats for rare plants, animals, birds and insects.

Our roller-coaster walk along heights that survey Covehurst Bay takes us to two ferny glens and on to the famous Dripping Well, a sylvan repose beloved by ramblers since Queen Victoria's day.

View from Fire Hills

Kiddiwalks in East Sussex

17

 Getting there *Fairlight is just 2 miles from the eastern outskirts of Hastings. Follow the A259 from Hastings seafront north-east for about 1¹/₂ miles to Ore and fork right just past the lights and the church on the left. The Hastings Country Park car park is signposted off to the right.*

Length of walk 3¹/₂ miles.
Time 3 hours.
Terrain Well-maintained footpaths and steps but the steepness of some of the climbs precludes younger children.
Start/Parking Park free in the Hastings Country Park car park (GR 859117). Toilet facilities are available in the top car park nearest the road.
Map OS Explorer 124 Hastings and Bexhill.

Refreshments At the start of the walk is the inviting Coastguards Tea Room – home-made cakes, cream teas and light lunches. Open Wednesday to Sunday. Telephone: 01424 812902.

❶ Leave the top car park and, opposite the entrance, follow the sign to the café. Go right on the lane and proceed forward over the bottom car park onto Fire Hills. (*Note the plaque on the left commemorating the Hastings-born conservation pioneer Grey Owl.*) Continue on the lane passing the cottages and go through a gate at the side of the Coastguards Station and Radar Tower.

❷ Turn right and go forward through a kissing gate. Drop down and swing left down the steps. Cross the stream in Warren

◆ Fun Things to See and Do ◆

See the Genesis Triptych in **St Andrew's church** in Fairlight (left of the door) and the stupendous view from the top of its tower, which was opened to the public in 1970. On a clear day, you can spot Boulogne in France!
The breezy cliffs are perfect for **kite flying**.

The Walk

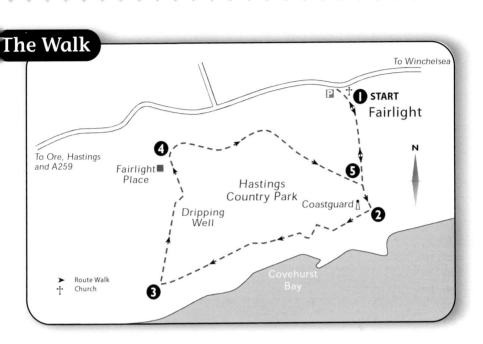

Glen and keep going forward uphill into the wood, following the sign to Fairlight Glen. Mount the steps and descend left, swinging right downhill into the bottom and cross the stream in Fairlight Glen.

3 Turn right, following the footpath sign to Barley Lane uphill, and work your way up to the Dripping Well. Keep forward from here and veer off right, swinging right to a gate, going right and left past Place Farm and Fairlight Place.

4 Turn right, following a footpath sign through a kissing gate. Continue forward to the cottage, veering right and heading toward the Coastguards Station.

5 Turn left on the outward route back to the starting point.

Kiddiwalks in East Sussex

◆ Background Notes ◆

Fairlight church stands at a height of 536 ft above sea level, its tower giving an extra 82 feet of view. The tower was built to the specifications of the Ministry of Defence and is a prominent landmark for vessels rounding South Foreland and Beachy Head. From the top you can see France and the UK coastal towns of Rye, Dungeness and Folkstone. At one time, observers could see 70 martello towers, 66 churches, 40 windmills, 5 castles and 3 bays! In the 13th century St Andrew's was a place of sanctuary for fugitives.

Fire Hills is so called because its gorse seems like a golden conflagration when viewed by mariners from the sea.

Grey Owl, Archibald Stansfeld Belaney (1888–1938), was born and educated in Hastings. He became fascinated with North American Indian culture and went to live among the tribes, integrating fully in their ways and developing an enormous respect for the natural world. He adopted the name Grey Owl and campaigned vigorously on environmental issues until his death. *Grey Owl*, a recent film about his life, starred Pierce Brosnan.

Local artist **Marianne North**, daughter of a Hastings MP, is noted for her canvases of local wild flowers, many of her pictures gracing the botanical archives at Kew.

Kiddies on Covehurst Bay Sands

18

♦ ♦

Brightling Down

Fuller's Earth

Footbridge in Forge Wood.

He's been dead since 1834 but former MP John Fuller of Brightling continues to cast a magical spell over a beautiful part of East Sussex that announces itself to the newcomer in a series of follies. 'What's that?' I gasped as I drove along the leafy lanes, observing a mausoleum (his!) that would grace Egypt's Valley of the Kings, an obelisk that stands on the second highest point in the county, an imposing celestial observatory and a conical-shaped extravagance known as the Sugar Loaf that, legend supposes, was raised in one night to win a bet! The spirit of John Fuller, variously known as 'Mad Jack', 'Honest Jack' or the 'Hippopotamus', still dominates this area of woods and rolling hillsides. Our walk at the edge of Brightling Down through Sugarloaf Wood, Long Wood and Forge Wood affords views of two of the old eccentric's creations.

This labyrinthine ramble through glades awash with bluebells in the spring is a sensual delight in all seasons, dappled sunlight, the calls of rare birds, the tinkle of streams and the pungent aromas of pine combining to create a memorable 'lost in the woods' Hansel and Gretel experience. Our route passes through a dell that once sounded to the ring of forge hammers. All is now tranquillity itself.

Kiddiwalks in East Sussex

◆ Fun Things to See and Do ◆

Follow the Fuller trail and see the **Sugar Loaf** – a few hundred yards east of the Swan Inn down a footpath – the **Observatory** and the **Obelisk**, both of the latter around a mile north of Wood's Corner alongside the Wood's Corner to Burwash road. Another of his follies is a gloomy and mysterious structure known as the **Tower** – south-east of Brightling off the Brightling–Darwell road opposite Brightling Park. It can be viewed from a footpath. But his mausoleum (the **Pyramid** in St Thomas à Becket's church in Brightling) is the most impressive – go north from Wood's Corner and fork right, turning right again to the church.

Just up the road from Wood's Corner – take the lane opposite the pub and go north, fork left and take the next signposted left turn, then follow the signs eastwards along the A265 through Burwash and right to **Bateman's** – you will discover the former home of Rudyard Kipling. He bought the former iron master's property in 1902 and stayed until 1936. Every child on the planet must have heard of his *Jungle Book*? This wonderful house set in a magnificent garden partly designed by the author himself was built in sandstone in 1634. It was bequeathed to the nation upon Kipling's death and is now owned by the National Trust. They have lovingly preserved the property and its contents including the evocative study where *Puck of Pook's Hill* and *Rewards and Fairies* were written. Children have a special guidebook to the house and gardens, putting them on the trail of Mowgli, Shere Khan and the other characters who were so wonderfully brought to life by Kipling's father – an accomplished artist in his own right. Bateman's superb grounds accommodate an old corn mill recently restored, youngsters having the opportunity of trying their hands at grinding using miniature grindstones. There is a café in the grounds serving lunches, snacks and teas. Open during the spring and summer seasons – telephone 01435 882302 for opening times.

Brightling Down

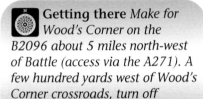

Getting there *Make for Wood's Corner on the B2096 about 5 miles north-west of Battle (access via the A271). A few hundred yards west of Wood's Corner crossroads, turn off southwards towards Dallington.*

Length of walk $3^1/_2$ miles.
Time 3 hours.
Terrain Woodland and field paths with short inclines and frequent stiles. In places the tracks are overgrown and a little scratchy for young legs. The route is a complicated one with few landmarks and direction signs are infrequent. In parts, it's not as shown on the OS map.
Start/Parking Immediately off the main road, park on the hill verge next to the telephone kiosk opposite the lane end and Carrick Farm (GR 662194).
Map OS Explorer 124 Hastings and Bexhill.
Refreshments The 14th century Swan Inn at the Wood's Corner crossroads offers a good selection of bar meals, specialising in locally caught fish and farm fresh produce. It has an attractive beer garden with long distance views. Telephone: 01424 838242.

---

1 Cross the road and walk down the lane past Carrick Farm, continuing to the four-directions signboard. On the skyline to the right are views of the Observatory and the Obelisk.

2 Go right following the directional arrow of the third sign (when viewed clockwise from left to right), following the track downhill to Highlands Farm through the woods. Just before the house, turn right following a footpath sign and cross a footbridge over a stream in the bottom, going left uphill and right away from the stream, proceeding through a conifer plantation. Go right along a track ascending left to a second track. Go left for 40 yards and turn right over a footbridge and go left. At the direction sign, weave right following a wood edge path, swinging right to a stile.

3 Cross into a field and follow the hedge down to a second stile. Cross and follow a second hedge down to a third stile.

4 Go sharp left over the stile into a field and cross a fourth stile back into the wood. Drop down the steps to a footbridge and

18

The Walk

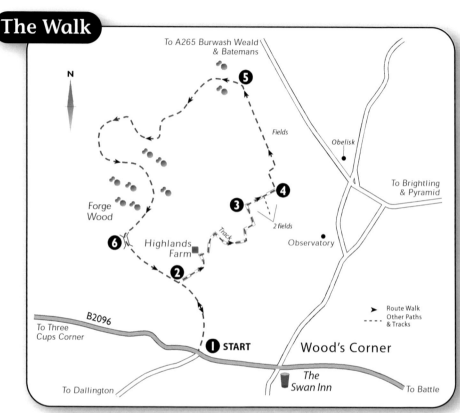

weave right uphill to a fifth stile. Cross into a meadow and steer left to a sixth stile, crossing a footbridge, and a seventh stile, aiming left over the next field to the edge of the wood.

5 Cross an eighth stile into the wood and swing left on the broad path. Drop down, swinging in a loop right. Swing left to join a track and go right. At the fork, go left and drop down to a footpath marker by two horizontal fence rails. Go left, following the direction posts through the woods, swinging right. Drop down to a footbridge and swing right, following the direction marker over another footbridge, and swing right across a planked bridge. Take the right hand fork through the dell and drop down the steps to a substantial footbridge, crossing and going right for 20 yards at the three-direction sign, passing the three bollards to a track.

6 Go immediately left off the track, following a bridleway sign, and return to the four-direction sign. Turn right back to the starting point.

Last resting place of 'Mad Jack'

◆ Background Notes ◆

While he was away from his estate in London, Fuller boasted, for a bet, that he could see the spire of Dallington church from his estate. When he arrived home, however, he almost had to eat his words. The spire was not visible so, in a night, he arranged for the erection of the **Sugar Loaf**, a conical shaped eminence that had the desired effect. It has an entrance porch and several windows and was used for many years as a private residence. The **Observatory** had a more practical purpose. It was completed in 1818 and was used for astronomy. Using telescopes, servants could spy the squire from afar and rush to get the dinner on! The building is now a private house. The **Obelisk** or **Brightling Needle** is 646 feet above sea level. It was probably built to celebrate Wellington's victory over Napoleon in 1815. It has recently been repaired. The **Tower** is 35 feet high with four windows and a battlemented top. It may have been built to enable Fuller to keep a watching eye on repairs to Bodiam Castle – he saved the castle from demolition. By far the most compelling and intriguing folly for children is Fuller's monumental tomb known as the **Pyramid**. It is 25 feet high, built in the grand tradition of the pharaohs. You can look inside and wonder if the old tradition is true. The top-hatted squire in full evening attire is supposed, by some, to have been interred sitting at an old iron table with a wonderful meal and a bottle of his favourite claret before him. At 22 stones he liked his grub!

19

Forest Row

Flowers of the Forest

The ruins of Brambletye House

Setting out from a lively village at the edge of Ashdown Forest, this exciting nature ramble orbits the ghostly ruins of Brambletye House, threading a labyrinthine circuit round the old moat, through meadows and woods and back along an abandoned railway line.

Young ramblers will enjoy the profusion of flowers along the way. Springtime primroses and bluebells are a particular delight and our path visits a badger sett, birdsong accompanying us along the entire route.

The area has a colourful history to animate any youngster!

Getting there *The starting point is the centre of Forest Row, a small town about 4 miles south-east of East Grinstead on the A22 Brighton to London road.*

Length of walk 3³/₄ miles.
Time 3 hours.
Terrain Undulating field paths and a level old railway track.
Start/Parking The walk begins just north of the church in the centre of Forest Row opposite the Chequers Inn hotel. There is a car park 200 yards south-east of the centre off Hartfield Road, which begins opposite the church (GR 427350).
Map OS Explorer 135 Ashdown Forest.
Refreshments There are a number of refreshment options in Forest Row. Conveniently sited in The Square at the start of this walk is an attractive old coaching inn – the Chequers Inn hotel, built in 1452. It offers popular roast-filled ciabattas and traditional roasts, daily specials including dishes such as bacon and brie omelette and tagliatelle carbonara. Telephone: 01342 823333.

◆ Fun Things to See and Do ◆

 Part of this walk uses an abandoned railway line, many families with young children hiring bikes – some with attached rickshaw type buggies – to enjoy a traffic free experience along the **Forest Way Cycle Trail**. Bike hire and full details from Future Cycles Bike Hire, 500 yards from the trail in Lower Square, Forest Row. Telephone: 01342 822847.

Around 2¹/₂ miles south of Forest Row at Wych Cross on the A22, just south of the junction with the A275, is the **Ashdown Forest Llama Park**, a herd of over 100 llamas and alpacas providing an irresistible attraction for children. The park has a museum, a picnic area with an adventure playground, an Alpaca Shop and a café. Open all year round. Telephone: 01825 712040.

Kiddiwalks in East Sussex

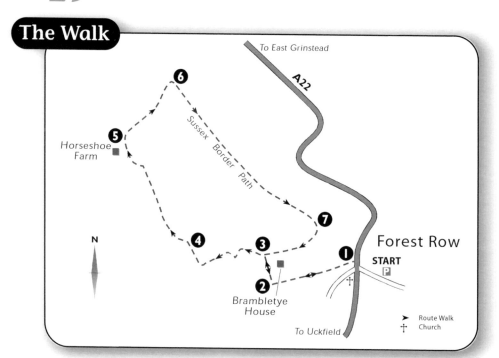

19

The Walk

To East Grinstead

A22

Sussex Border Path

Horseshoe Farm

Forest Row

START
P

Brambletye House

To Uckfield

➤ Route Walk
✝ Church

N

❶ Cross the London Road from the Chequers Inn hotel and go though an archway in a modern development, following a footpath sign. Drop down the steps and follow a winding path left, then go right, leaving the village, heading up to a stile. Cross into a field and walk down the hedgeline to the corner. Cross a stile right, followed by a stile left between the barns and then go immediately left again over a further stile, turning right on a path. Drop down to a stile and cross into a field, heading

left. Looming on the right are the remains of Brambletye House. Cross a stile and go slightly left between a new plantation and walk on to a stile, crossing to the old bridge.

❷ Turn right over the bridge – it's a wonderful perch for playing pooh sticks and no tourists! Go forward 50 yards and swing left and right between the old moated area. On the right is an overgrown but intriguing tunnel. Continue to the lane.

Young cyclists along the route

❸ Turn left on the lane and swing left and right in front of Brambletye Barn. *There is a good view of the moat to the left. Immediately to the left of the lane, masked by modern brickwork, is an original arched bridge. In the garden of the barn conversion are fragments of an old building.* Climb and swing right to the neck of a wood.

❹ Swing right into the bluebell wood. *Halfway along is a multiple-entranced badger sett. Tread quietly, they're asleep!* Leave the wood and follow the footpath sign up right across a field. At the edge, follow a footpath sign over a stile, swinging left and going right by Horseshoe Farm.

❺ Go right on the lane to the bridge.

6 Turn right along the line of the abandoned railway for just under a mile.

7 Turn right at Brambletye Crossing and pass the imposing monumental entrance to Brambletye House, returning to outward point 3. Turn left on the outward route back to the starting point.

◆ Background Notes ◆

From the 1200s **Ashdown Forest** was a preserve of kings, the royal reserve providing hunting for deer and wild boar. Hunting lodges were built near Forest Row and elsewhere, the MP Sir Henry Compton erecting his **Brambletye House** to an Italian design in 1631. It had a moat filled by the waters of the River Medway. The author Horace Smith wrote a historical romance *Brambletye House*, which was praised by Sir Walter Scott. Compton was accused of high treason and escaped to Spain in 1683, the mansion's subsequent owner allowing the property to fall into disrepair.

Forest Row was once a very dangerous area for vulnerable and undefended travellers. **Highwaymen** plied its lucrative Brighton to London road. In 1801, two local brigands, the Beatson brothers, held up a stagecoach at gunpoint. They were arrested, tried in Horsham and returned to the scene of their crime for execution. A gallows was erected in Forest Row and the men were hanged on 7th April 1802 before a crowd of three thousand. As part of their learning a healthy respect for the law, local boys would be made to touch the corpses!

20
East Dean

Genuine Crowlink

The Tiger Inn at East Dean

The pretty, award winning village of East Dean snuggles in a fold of the Downs, its circle of old cottages, ancient church and low-beamed inn completing a quintessentially English idyll that draws artists and photographers and those footloose visitors who just want to quaff and linger awhile. An agricultural community, producing high grade lamb – with, at one time, plenty of illicit French gin and brandy to wash it down – the village is just a short walk from the sea and a topographical wonder that could well be the national emblem.

This giddy walk through the National Trust estate known as Crowlink ascends the downland heights, pulled all the way by the magnetic vision of the Belle Tout lighthouse. It takes us to the tiny landfall of Birling Gap and on to the see-saw ride that is a traverse of the magnificent Seven Sisters cliffs before returning over meadows brimming with flowers in summer.

Kiddiwalks in East Sussex

20

Getting there *East Dean is on the A259 between Eastbourne and Seaford.*

Length of walk 4 miles.
Time 4 hours.
Terrain Woodland paths and mostly turfy tracks but the rolling ascents and descents may well be too taxing for very young legs.
Start/Parking Park in the East Dean Community Centre car park – off Birling Gap Road, 180 yards south of the A259 junction (GR 557977).

Map OS Explorer 123 Eastbourne and Beachy Head.
Refreshments The Birling Gap Hotel offers a range of bar meals including locally caught cod and plaice. Telephone: 01323 423197. The recommended Tiger Inn in East Dean (show the children the real tiger's head in the bar) also serves excellent local produce including game in season. Eating outside almost on the village green is such fun! Telephone: 01323 423209.

◆ Fun Things to See and Do ◆

The most adventurous first! When the wind is in the right quarter and the waves are up, good surfing can be had at **Birling Gap**. Rock pooling and fossil hunting can also be enjoyed here although the beach is predominantly composed of pebbles.

Just down the road from East Dean (further along Birling Gap Road) is a centre voted the 'Best Family Attraction in Sussex', the **Seven Sisters Sheep Centre**, housed in a 17th-century flint barn, allowing children to get up close and personal with new born lambs, pigs, goats, calves, rabbits and chicks and to experience shearing, spinning, milking and cheese making. Boasting 40 different breeds of sheep, the centre has probably the largest collection in the world. It also provides a tea room and a gift shop. Open every day from March to September. Telephone: 01323 423302.

The Walk

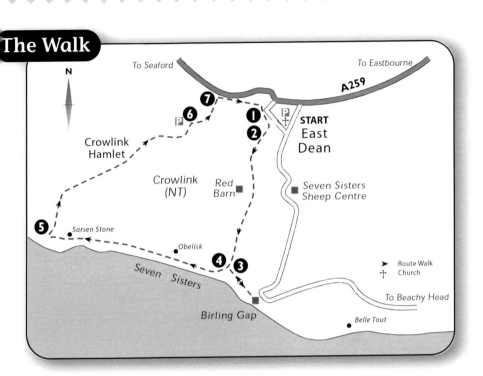

1 Walk away from the village hall and leave the car park in the top left hand corner, turning right to the village green and the Tiger Inn. Go left over the green to Upper Street. Turn left, taking the right hand fork, Went Way, following the no through road sign. Pass the old village school. Continue on the lane to Went Acre.

2 Go through a gate onto a footpath and ascend a rise, going left to a gate. Enter the National Trust estate of Crowlink. Walk uphill through the wood and emerge from the trees, merging right with a path. Head for the Red Barn on Went Hill. Pass the barn and keep to the right of the windswept trees and bushes and veer right to pick up a broad green track. Walk on to a gate. Go through and keep forward to the next gate. Go through, continuing on a stony path to the direction signs.

3 Keep forward here and go left on a track to Birling Gap. Retrace your steps to the end of point 2.

4 Go left, following the South Downs Way sign. Go through a kissing gate onto downland. Descend to the obelisk. Continue over the undulating cliffs to the sarsen stone. Drop down.

A friendly scarecrow.

5 Turn right at the bottom on a green track heading in the direction of Gayles, the mansion on the hill in the far distance. Swing right at the stile (don't cross) and follow the hedge right to a gate. Go through and keep walking forward into the hamlet of Crowlink. Keep forward and merge with a lane, climbing left to a gate and a parking area.

6 Go over a stile to the right of the gate and head diagonally right across the meadow to a gate. Go through and keep forward along the field edge to the corner.

7 Turn right through the flower meadow called Hobb's Eares and continue into East Dean. Turn right and left back to the parking area.

The **school** mentioned at point 1 was used to accommodate children evacuated from the blitz-vulnerable London borough of Rotherhithe during World War Two.

Erosion is a constant problem at **Birling Gap**. The missing seaward portion of the old coastguard cottages on the left succumbed in 1968. Birling Gap was a convenient landing point for contraband and smuggling gangs operated in the area for decades. The trade, which involved even local vicars and men of standing, was almost fashionable. Genuine Crowlink was a euphemism for smuggled gin of the finest quality and provenance!

One vicar who no doubt liked a tipple or two was **Jonathan Darby** of East Dean. Did he have a vested interest in excavating a cave with his own hands in the notorious cliff under Belle Tout and sitting there of an evening with a flaming lantern to warn sailors of the danger of shipwreck? The light in Darby's Hole famously saved many a mariner from a splintering death in the early 18th century. Darby died in 1726 and is buried in East Dean church. His flat-stoned tomb is to the right of the porch near the path. On 'Sea Sunday' in July, local people remember their 'Sailors' Friend' in a ceremony of wreath laying.

East Dean church has just one of a handful of surviving **tapsell gates** in the county. They open on a central spindle

The scintillating **Seven Sisters** were formed about 85 million years ago, consisting of the tiny skeletons of organisms that existed in a shallow sea.

This area is a haven for wildlife of every description. The wheatear, one little bird that thankfully still flourishes on these cliffs, was once captured by shepherds by the thousand as a supplement to their meagre incomes. It was regarded as a local delicacy.

Birds to see along the way

KINGFISHER

NIGHTINGALE

MALLARD

CURLEW

REDSHANK

COMMON TERN

HERON

DUNLIN

CORMORANT